standards for educational and psychological testing

American Educational Research Association
American Psychological Association
National Council on Measurement in Education

The *Standards for Educational and Psychological Testing* will be under continuing review by the three cooperating organizations. Comments and suggestions will be welcome and should be sent to The Committee to Develop Standards for Educational and Psychological Testing in care of The Executive Officer, The American Psychological Association, 1200 17th Street, NW, Washington, DC 20036.

The Library of Congress has cataloged this book as follows, and it is recommended that citations and reference entries reflect the LC cataloging.

Standards for educational and psychological testing. (1985). Washington, DC: American Psychological Association.

Prepared by the

Committee to Develop Standards for
Educational and Psychological Testing of
The American Educational Research Association,
The American Psychological Association, and
The National Council on Measurement in Education.

Melvin R. Novick, Chair

Copyright © 1985 by the
American Psychological Association

Reprinted May 1986

Published by the
American Psychological Association, Inc.
1200 Seventeenth Street, NW
Washington, DC 20036

Library of Congress Catalog Card Number 85-71493
ISBN 0-912704-95-0

Contents

Preface

There have been four earlier documents from three sponsoring organizations guiding the development and use of tests. The first of these was *Technical Recommendations for Psychological Tests and Diagnostic Techniques,* prepared by a committee of the American Psychological Association (APA) and published by that organization in 1954. The second was *Technical Recommendations for Achievement Tests,* prepared by a committee representing the American Educational Research Association (AERA) and the National Council on Measurement Used in Education and published by the National Education Association in 1955. The third, which replaced the earlier two, was published by APA in 1966 and prepared by a committee representing APA, AERA, and the National Council on Measurement in Education (NCME) and called *Standards for Educational and Psychological Tests and Manuals.* The fourth, a revision of the third document, which was prepared by the three sponsoring organizations, was published in 1974.

By 1977 it had become apparent that the 1974 publication was becoming outdated because of new problems and issues involving testing. Technical advances in testing and related fields, new and emerging uses of tests, and growing social concerns over the role of testing in achieving social goals indicated the need for a revision of the 1974 *Standards for Educational and Psychological Tests.* Consequently, the APA Committee on Psychological Tests and Assessment contacted AERA and NCME to form a joint committee to review the 1974 *Standards.* The review committee in due course issued a report recommending revision and outlining guidelines for that process. The review committee report was the basis for the charge to the Committee to Develop Standards for Educational and Psychological Testing.

The following guidelines, adapted from the Joint AERA, APA, NCME Review Committee's report (1979, pp. 12-13) have governed the work of the revision committee. The *Standards* should

1. Address issues of test use in a variety of applications.

2. Be a statement of technical standards for sound professional practice and not a social action prescription.

3. Make it possible to determine the technical adequacy of a test, the appropriateness and propriety of specific applications, and the reasonableness of inferences based on the test results.

4. Require that test developers, publishers, and users collect and make available sufficient information to enable a qualified reviewer to determine whether applicable standards were met.

5. Embody a strong ethical imperative, though it was understood that the *Standards* itself would not contain enforcement mechanisms.

6. Recognize that all standards will not be uniformly applicable across a wide range of instruments and uses.

7. Be presented at a level that would enable a wide range of people who work with tests or test results to use the *Standards.*

8. Not inhibit experimentation in the development, use, and interpretation of tests.

9. Reflect the current level of consensus of recognized experts.

10. Supersede the 1974 *Standards for Educational and Psychological Tests.*

The *Standards* has been produced by a committee appointed by the three sponsoring organizations. Members of the committee were

Lloyd Bond	Barbara M. Pedulla
John P. Campbell	Susan W. Sherman, Vice Chair
Goldine C. Gleser	Richard E. Snow
Robert L. Linn, Vice Chair	Carol Kehr Tittle
George F. Madaus	Concepcion M. Valadez
Melvin R. Novick, Chair	LaMonte G. Wyche

The late Ronald Edmonds served as a member of the joint committee in 1981. Professional staff associates were Catherine O'Bryant (August 1981 through August 1983), Debra Boltas (beginning August 1983), Robert P. Lowman (until August 1981), and Lisa M. Soule (until August 1981). Donald N. Bersoff served as legal counsel to the committee. The glossary and index were prepared with the assistance of T. Anne Cleary, Timothy Ansley, Stephen Dunbar, David Frisbie, and John Keene. Sheri Russell typed and processed the many drafts of the *Standards*. Finally, the help of the clerical and editorial support staff at APA is acknowledged. Partial financial support for this project was provided by the Carnegie Corporation of New York and the Russell Sage Foundation.

All committee members served in an individual professional capacity and not as representatives of any organization or institution. More than 125 people agreed to serve as advisers to the committee. Some were selected on the basis of their technical expertise, others because of their acquaintance with and involvement in the various controversies involving testing. Advisers to the committee include the following people:

Norman Abeles	Ronald K. Hambleton
Peter W. Airasian	Walter M. Haney
Earl A. Alluisi	Lenore W. Harmon
Anne Anastasi	Kathleen Heid
Scarvia Bateman Anderson	Edwin L. Herr
William H. Angoff	Albert N. Hieronymus
Steve Arvizu	Asa G. Hilliard
C. J. Bartlett	Laura M. Hines
Theodore H. Blau	John L. Holland
Virginia R. Boehm	Hiram D. Hoover
Robert K. Boruch	Charles L. Hulin
Frederick G. Brown	Lloyd G. Humphreys
Beverly Cabello	David Ihilevich
Arthur Canter	Gail H. Ironson
Joan B. Chase	Stephen H. Ivens
Helen J. Christrup	John H. Jackson
T. Anne Cleary	Richard M. Jaeger
Nancy S. Cole	Lyle V. Jones
Robert W. Consalvo	Joseph Kandor
William W. Cooley	Michael T. Kane
Lee J. Cronbach	Jerome T. Kapes
Bruce Davey	Mildred E. Katzell
George Dawson	Edward L. King, Jr.
Harold E. Dent	Gerald P. Koocher
Esther E. Diamond	Nadine M. Lambert
Jerome E. Doppelt	Luis M. Laosa
Fritz Drasgow	Roger T. Lennon
Marvin D. Dunnette	Arthur C. MacKinney
Richard P. Duran	Brendan A. Maher
Patricia J. Dyer	Ricardo A. Martinez
Robert L. Ebel	Joseph D. Matarazzo
Herbert W. Eber	John Mcnamara
Marion Epstein	Jane R. Mercer
Frank W. Erwin	Samuel J. Messick
Frank Evans	James Mitchell
Lorraine D. Eyde	Paul R. Munford
Frank H. Farley	Peter E. Nathan
Richard L. Ferguson	Rosemery O. Nelson
Richard A. Figueroa	Laurel W. Oliver
Fred L. Finch	Samuel H. Osipow
Thomas J. Fitzgibbon	James L. Outtz
Edwin A. Fleishman	Amado M. Padilla
Robert Glaser	Joseph J. Pedulla
Robert M. Guion	Nancy S. Petersen

W. James Popham
Charles A. Pounian
Dale J. Prediger
Diana Pullin
Marilyn K. Quaintance
Marjorie Ragosta
Daniel J. Reschly
Lauren B. Resnick
Cecil R. Reynolds
Donald K. Routh
Frank L. Schmidt
Donald J. Schwartz
Lee B. Sechrest
Wayne S. Sellman
Trevor E. Sewell
Loretta A. Shepard
Benjamin Shimberg
Virginia C. Shipman

Rodney W. Skager
Frank W. Snyder
C. Paul Sparks
Jack Spear
Charles F. Sproule
Daniel Stufflebeam
Mary L. Tenopyr
Robert L. Thorndike
Ann Miller Tiedemann
James Ward
William Webster
Herbert I. Weisberg
Douglas R. Whitney
E. Belvin Williams
Protase Woodford
James E. Ysseldyke
Donald G. Zytowski

Written comments were also received from many other people in the profession.

The later drafts of this document were reviewed by ad hoc committees representing the governing bodies of the sponsoring organizations. The following is a list of the members of these committees.

AERA ad hoc Committee of Council
Anne C. Petersen, Chair
Donald R. Warren
T. Anne Cleary

APA ad hoc Committee of Council
Virginia D. C. Bennett, Chair
Earl A. Alluisi
Anne Anastasi
Robert M. Guion
John H. Jackson
Samuel H. Osipow

Lee B. Sechrest
Milton F. Shore
Suzanne B. Sobel
Jack G. Wiggins, Jr.

NCME ad hoc Committee of the Board of Directors
Nancy S. Cole, President (1983-84)
George F. Madaus
Loretta A. Shepard

In preparing the *Standards,* the joint committee has taken cognizance of standards, guidelines, reports, principles, and policy statements issued by various organizations and also of the many criticisms of these documents. These documents are listed in the Bibliography. Some of the referenced documents address legal, social, and political issues in a substantive way and thus go beyond the domain of the technical standards. The *Standards,* however, addresses major current uses of tests, technical issues relating to a broad range of social and legal concerns, and the varied needs of all the participants in the testing process.

These standards were formulated with the intent of being consistent with the APA's *Ethical Principles of Psychologists* (1981). These principles are binding on members of APA. The committee suggests that those who are not members of APA consider the ethical principles to be advisory in general outline if not in detail. These standards were also formulated with the intent of being consistent with the APA *Standards for Providers of Psychological Services* (1977).

Committee to Develop Standards for
Educational and Psychological Testing

References

American Psychological Association. (1977). Standards for providers of psychological services. *American Psychologist,* 32(6), 495-505.

American Psychological Association. (1981). Ethical principles of psychologists. *American Psychologist,* 36(6), 633-638.

Joint AERA, APA, NCME Committee for Review of the Standards for Educational and Psychological Tests. (1979). *Report of the joint AERA, APA, NCME committee for review of the standards for educational and psychological tests.* Washington, DC: American Psychological Association.

Introduction

Educational and psychological testing represents one of the most important contributions of behavioral science to our society. It has provided fundamental and significant improvements over previous practices in industry, government, and education. It has provided a tool for broader and more equitable access to education and employment. Although not all tests are well-developed, nor are all testing practices wise and beneficial, available evidence supports the judgment of the Committee on Ability Testing of the National Research Council that the proper use of well-constructed and validated tests provides a better basis for making some important decisions about individuals and programs than would otherwise be available.

Educational and psychological testing has also been the target of extensive scrutiny, criticism, and debate both outside and within the professional testing community. The most frequent criticisms are that tests play too great a role in the lives of students and employees and that tests are biased and exclusionary. In consideration of these and other criticisms, the *Standards* is intended to provide a basis for evaluating the quality of testing practices as they affect the various parties involved.

Participants in the Testing Process

Educational and psychological testing involves and significantly affects individuals, institutions, and society as a whole. The individuals affected include students, parents, teachers, educational administrators, job applicants, employees, patients, supervisors, executives, and evaluators. The institutions affected include schools, colleges, businesses, industry, and government agencies. Individuals and institutions benefit when testing helps them achieve their goals. Society, in turn, benefits when the achievement of individual and institutional goals contributes to the general good.

The interests of the various parties in the testing process are usually, but not always, congruent. For example, when a test is given for counseling purposes or for job placement, the interests of the individual and the institution often coincide. However, when a test is used to select from among many individuals for a highly competitive job or educational or training program, the preferences of an applicant may be inconsistent with those of an employer or admissions officer.

There are generally three main participants in the testing process: the *test developer,* who develops, publishes, markets, and often administers and scores the test; the *test user,* who requires the test results for some decision-making purpose; and the *test taker,* who takes the test by choice, direction, or necessity. Often there is a *test sponsor,* which may be a board that represents institutions or a governmental agency, that contracts with a test developer for a specific instrument or service. In addition there may also be a *test administrator,* who handles the actual administration of the test, and a *test reviewer,* who conducts a scholarly review to evaluate the suitability of the test for the uses proposed.

The roles of test developer, test taker, test user, and test sponsor are sometimes combined and sometimes further divided. In counseling, the test taker is typically the primary user of the test results. Sometimes the test administrator is an agent of the test developer, and sometimes the test administrator is also the test user. When an industrial organization prepares its own employment tests, it is both the developer and the user. Sometimes a test is developed by a test author but published, advertised, and distributed by an independent publisher, though in most cases the publisher plays an active role in the test development.

The Purpose of These Standards

Recent controversies over testing make the development of the *Standards* vitally important to all participants in the testing process. Many issues need to be addressed in a way that does not preempt the political process. In general, the *Standards* advocates that, within feasible limits, the necessary technical information be made available so that those involved in policy debate may be fully informed. The *Standards* does not attempt to provide psychometric answers to policy questions. However, complete separation of scientific and social concerns is not possible. The requirement in

1

the *Standards* for documentation and scientific analysis may sometimes, in itself, place a greater burden on one side of a policy issue than on another.

The purpose of publishing the *Standards* is to provide criteria for the evaluation of tests, testing practices, and the effects of test use. Although the evaluation of the appropriateness of a test or application should depend heavily on professional judgment, the *Standards* can provide a frame of reference to assure that relevant issues are addressed. The *Standards* does not attempt to assign precise responsibility for the satisfaction of individual standards. To do so would be difficult, especially since much work in testing is done by contractual arrangement. However, all professional test developers, sponsors, publishers, and users should make reasonable efforts to observe the *Standards* and to encourage others to do so.

The *Standards* is not meant to prescribe the use of specific statistical methods. Where specific statistical reporting requirements are mentioned, the phrase "or equivalent" should always be understood. For concreteness, the standards sometimes refer to a common method of achieving specific reporting objectives. In particular situations, however, more desirable alternatives may be available.

Cautions To Be Exercised in Using These Standards

The *Standards* is a technical guide that can be used as the basis for evaluating testing practices. Evaluating the acceptability of a test or test application does not rest on the literal satisfaction of every primary standard in this document, and acceptability cannot be determined by using a checklist. Specific circumstances affect the importance of individual standards. Individual standards should not be considered in isolation. Therefore, evaluating acceptability involves the following: professional judgment that is based on a knowledge of behavioral science, psychometrics, and the professional field to which the tests apply; the degree to which the intent of this document has been satisfied by the test developer and user; the alternatives that are readily available; and research and experiential evidence regarding feasibility.

The use of the standards in litigation is inevitable; it should be emphasized, however, that in legal proceedings and elsewhere professional judgment based on the accepted corpus of knowledge always plays an essential role in determining the relevance of particular standards in particular situations. The *Standards* is intended to offer guidance for such judgments.

It would not be appropriate for test developers or test users to state that a test, manual, or procedure satisfies or follows these standards. That judgment is more appropriately made by others in the professional community.

These standards are concerned with a field that is evolving. Therefore, there is a continuing need for monitoring and revising this document as knowledge develops. There are some areas in which new developments are particularly likely, such as gender-specific or combined-gender norms, cultural bias, computer based test interpretation, validity generalization, differential prediction, and flagging test scores for people with handicapping conditions.

Categories of Standards

In previous versions of the *Standards,* the classifications "essential," "highly desirable," and "desirable" were used to indicate the relative importance of the individual standards. In the 1985 *Standards,* new categories and labels are used, in part to avoid the troublesome distinction between desirable and highly desirable and to avoid the label "essential." The standards are now categorized either as being of primary or of secondary importance. Importance is viewed largely as a function of the potential impact that the testing process has on individuals, institutions, and society.

Primary standards are those that should be met by all tests before their operational use and in all test uses, unless a sound professional reason is available to show why it is not necessary, or technically feasible, to do so in a particular case. Test developers and users and, where appropriate, sponsors, are expected to be able to explain why any primary standards have not been met.

Secondary standards are desirable as goals but are likely to be beyond reasonable expectation in many situations. Although careful consideration of these standards will often be helpful in evaluating tests and programs and in comparing the usefulness of competing instruments, limitations on resources may make adherence to them infeasible in many situations. Some secondary standards describe procedures that are beneficial but not often used. Test developers and users are not expected to be able to explain why secondary standards have not been met.

The importance of some standards for test construction and evaluation will vary with application. These standards are designated as *conditional*. Such standards should be considered primary for some situations and secondary for others. In deciding whether to take an individual conditional standard as primary or secondary, one should consider carefully the feasibility of meeting that standard in relation to the potential consequences to all parties involved in the testing process. It may be infeasible technically or financially for some testing programs to observe some conditional standards, particularly those programs that conduct low-volume tests. However, if the use of a test is likely to have serious consequences for test takers, especially if a large number of people may be affected, conditional standards assume increased importance.

The categories in which standards are placed should be viewed as imperfect. Where testing has a limited role in a larger assessment procedure (e.g., tests conducted by a clinical, industrial, or school psychologist), some primary standards, especially those dealing with documentation, should be considered as having a secondary designation.

Ideally all relevant primary standards should be met at publication or first operational use of each test. Because the development of a test for widespread use is an extensive undertaking, a requirement that all relevant primary standards be satisfied at first operational use would be likely to stifle both the development of new instruments and progress in the field. Furthermore, a testing professional who is put in charge of a new or continuing program that does not meet relevant primary standards cannot be expected to remedy all that program's shortcomings immediately.

When judging the short-term acceptability of a test or program under development or redevelopment, the test user should determine that the test is on a par with readily available alternatives. In addition, the test developer or publisher should determine that

1. advertising for a test or program recommends only applications supported by the test's research base;

2. necessary cautions are given in the manual or elsewhere to encourage sufficiently limited reliance on the test results, particularly when the use of the new test will have significant impact on the test takers; and

3. there is clear indication of continuing and significant improvement in the research base directed toward observance of the standards.

Tests and Test Uses to Which These Standards Apply

The major new sections in the 1985 *Standards* relate to test use. The *Standards* emphasizes that test users should have a sound technical and professional basis for their actions, much of which can be derived from research done by test developers and publishers. In selecting a test, a potential user should depend heavily upon the developer's research documentation that is clearly related to the intended application. Although the test developer should supply the needed information, the ultimate responsibility for appropriate test use lies with the user.

Tests include standardized ability (aptitude and achievement) instruments, diagnostic and evaluative devices, interest inventories, personality inventories, and projective instruments. The 1966 and 1974 *Standards* noted that the same general types of information are needed for all these varieties of published diagnostic, prognostic, and evaluative devices. Similarly, a more appropriate choice among assessment devices and subsequent use will be facilitated if there is reasonable comparability in the kinds of information made available to users.

In the *Standards* three broad categories of test instruments are covered: constructed performance tasks, questionnaires, and to a lesser extent, structured behavior samples. Constructed performance tasks are designed to isolate and assess particular educational and psychological constructs without having to simulate actual environmental or social situations in which such constructs are typically expressed. Printed answer sheets and pencil are the mediums most often used; however, oral exchange, oral recordings, and manipulatable objects form parts of some individually administered tests, and computerized test administration is becoming increasingly common. The performance tasks are often designed to be interpreted as maximum performance assessments. Conventional standardized ability tests are the most common examples. There are also constructed performance measures of some cognitive style and personality constructs.

Questionnaires and inventories are designed to provide a convenient medium through which people can be asked to report personal opinions, interests, attitudes, and typical reactions to situations and problems that have been or might be faced in everyday life. Personality or interest inventories, composed of lists of printed questions that the respondent answers by checking a defined degree of agreement or interest, are the most common examples.

Observable behavior can also be sampled directly to provide systematic, standardized assessments of personal skills and styles relevant to clinical, employment, and educational decision making. Such tests are called structured behavior sample tests. Social skills, speaking and writing skills, and the skills involved in artistic expression are examples of performance domains in which structured behavior samples have been used. Job sample tests have been used often in industry and in the military. Writing samples are now used widely in education. Tests of characteristic styles of performance under stress, in the face of complexity, or in situations where leadership is required provide other examples. Sometimes structured behavior samples are taken by observing behavior in real-world situations. In other instances, such situations are simulated to aid in standardization or for reasons of economy.

The need for reasonable comparability of the information provided to users is particularly compelling for the new uses of computers in testing that are being developed. Instruments developed initially in paper-and-pencil or interview form are being administered, scored, and in some instances, interpreted, by computers. There are also computerized adaptive tests and interviews. Although in some instances specific standards have been stated for tests administered by computer, all the standards apply with equal force to such tests. In many instances, the switch from paper and pencil to computer assessment will require additional evidence that relevant standards have been met in the new testing mode.

Although these standards apply primarily to constructed performance tasks, questionnaires, and structured behavior samples, they may also be usefully applied in varying degrees to the entire range of assessment techniques. It will generally not be possible, however, to apply the standards with the same rigor to the broad range of unstructured behavior samples that are used in some forms of clinical and school psychological assessment and to instructor-made tests that are used to evaluate student performance in education and training.

The term "test" usually refers to measures of either the constructed performance or structured behavior sample type, in which test takers are expected or instructed to try their best. Instruments for identifying interests and personality characteristics through self-report are typically and properly entitled "inventories," "questionnaires," or "checklists" rather than tests. In textual material, such as in the *Standards*, these self-report instruments may be called tests in order to simplify the language. They are called tests here to indicate that the standards also apply to these instruments. The term "test" should generally be avoided, however, in describing such instruments, especially in their titles.

Organization of This Volume

Part I of the *Standards,* "Technical Standards for Test Construction and Evaluation," contains standards for validity, reliability, test development, scaling, norming, comparability, equating, and publication. Part II presents "Professional Standards for Test Use." Part III, "Standards For Particular Applications," contains standards for testing linguistic minorities and people with handicapping conditions. The technical and professional standards discussed in Parts I and II are relevant to the particular applications in Part III. Part IV, "Standards for Administrative Procedures," contains standards regarding test administration, scoring, and reporting, as well as standards for the protection of test takers' rights. Although all four parts deal with technical issues, each also addresses how technical issues, professional practice, and professional ethics interface. The interface of standards with issues of professional practice is most evident in Part II and that with professional ethics in Part IV.

Each chapter begins with introductory text that provides background for the standards that follow. This text is meant to assist in the interpretation of the standards, not to impose additional standards. Many of the standards are followed by comments. These comments are not meant to impose additional requirements, only to explain the standards they follow.

The *Standards* also contains a glossary, a bibliography, and an index. The glossary provides definitions for terms as they are used in this volume specifically.

Part I

Technical Standards for Test Construction and Evaluation

1. Validity

Background

Validity is the most important consideration in test evaluation. The concept refers to the appropriateness, meaningfulness, and usefulness of the specific inferences made from test scores. Test validation is the process of accumulating evidence to support such inferences. A variety of inferences may be made from scores produced by a given test, and there are many ways of accumulating evidence to support any particular inference. Validity, however, is a unitary concept. Although evidence may be accumulated in many ways, validity always refers to the degree to which that evidence supports the inferences that are made from the scores. The inferences regarding specific uses of a test are validated, not the test itself.

Traditionally, the various means of accumulating validity evidence have been grouped into categories called *content-related, criterion-related,* and *construct-related evidence of validity*. These categories are convenient, as are other more refined categorizations (e.g., the division of the criterion-related category into predictive and concurrent evidence of validity), but the use of the category labels does not imply that there are distinct types of validity or that a specific validation strategy is best for each specific inference or test use. Rigorous distinctions between the categories are not possible. Evidence identified usually with the criterion-related or content-related categories, for example, is relevant also to the construct-related category.

An ideal validation includes several types of evidence, which span all three of the traditional categories. Other things being equal, more sources of evidence are better than fewer. However, the quality of the evidence is of primary importance, and a single line of solid evidence is preferable to numerous lines of evidence of questionable quality. Professional judgment should guide the decisions regarding the forms of evidence that are most necessary and feasible in light of the intended uses of the test and any likely alternatives to testing.

Resources should be invested in obtaining the combination of evidence that optimally reflects the value of a test for an intended purpose. In some circumstances, evidence pertaining to test content is critical; in others, criterion-related evidence is critical. Evidence regarding the psychological meaning of the construct is usually relevant and may become the central issue.

Gathering evidence may sometimes involve examining not only the present instrument in the present situation, but also the available evidence on the use of the same or similar instruments in similar situations. This process involves generalization, either on the basis of common elements, as in synthetic validation, or on the basis of overall job similarity, as in validity generalization.

Construct-Related Evidence

The evidence classed in the construct-related category focuses primarily on the test score as a measure of the psychological characteristic of interest. Reasoning ability, spatial visualization, and reading comprehension are constructs, as are personality characteristics such as sociability and introversion. Endurance is a frequently used construct in athletics. Studies of leadership behavior often refer to constructs such as consideration for subordinates (giving praise, explaining reasons for action, asking opinions) and initiating structure (setting goals, keeping on schedule). Such characteristics are referred to as constructs because they are theoretical constructions about the nature of human behavior. It should be noted that establishing the validity of a measure of a construct is a problem distinct from that of using that measure in predicting a second measure, although the latter can often contribute to construct validation.

The construct of interest for a particular test should be embedded in a conceptual framework, no matter how imperfect that framework may be.

The conceptual framework specifies the meaning of the construct, distinguishes it from other constructs, and indicates how measures of the construct should relate to other variables.

The process of compiling construct-related evidence for test validity starts with test development and continues until the pattern of empirical relationships between test scores and other variables clearly indicates the meaning of the test score. Especially when multiple measures of a construct are not available--as in many practical testing applications-- validating inferences about a construct also requires paying careful attention to aspects of measurement such as test format, administration conditions, or language level, that may affect test meaning and interpretation materially.

Evidence for the construct interpretation of a test may be obtained from a variety of sources. Intercorrelations among items may be used to support the assertion that a test measures primarily a single construct. Substantial relationships of a test to other measures that are purportedly of the same construct and the weaknesses of relationships to measures that are purportedly of different constructs support both the identification of constructs and distinctions among them. Relationships among different methods of measurement and among various nontest variables similarly sharpen and elaborate the meaning and interpretation of constructs.

Another line of evidence derives from analyses of individual responses. Questioning test takers about their performance strategies or responses to particular items or asking raters about the reasons for their ratings can yield hypotheses that enrich the definition of a construct. Theoretical models of psychological processes involved in the construct can be developed and evaluated by analyzing test scores. Furthermore, evidence from content- and criterion-related validation studies, which is described in the following sections, contributes to construct interpretations. The choice of which of one or more approaches to use to gather evidence for interpreting constructs--those described here or others--will depend on the particular validation problem and the extent to which validation is focused on construct meaning.

Content-Related Evidence

In general, content-related evidence demonstrates the degree to which the sample of items, tasks, or questions on a test are representative of some defined universe or domain of content. The methods often rely on expert judgments to assess the relationship between parts of the test and the defined universe, but certain logical and empirical procedures can also be used. For example, the major facets of a domain of academic subject matter can be specified, and experts in that subject can be asked to assign test items to the categories defined by those facets. The representativeness of the sample of items can then be judged. Sometimes algorithms or rules can be constructed to generate items that differ systematically on various domain facets, thus assuring representativeness.

As another example, systematic observations of behavior in a job may be combined with expert judgments to construct a representative or critical sample of the job domain, which then can be administered under standardized conditions in an off-the-job setting. Expert judgments can sometimes be used to assess the relative importance or criticality of various parts of a job, instructional program, or an item universe (e.g., identifying aspects of job performance that are critical in preventing accidents). A job sample test can then be made to cover those aspects more thoroughly. Also, if some aspects of the job are judged relatively unimportant, they may be excluded from the test.

The first task for test developers is to specify adequately the universe of content that a test is intended to represent, given the proposed uses of the test. When test users consider using an available test for a purpose other than that for which the test was developed originally, they need to judge the appropriateness of the original domain definition for the proposed new use. For some educational decisions, it is important to determine the agreement between the test and the curricular or instructional domains it is meant to cover.

Another important task is to determine the degree to which the format and response properties of the sample of items or tasks in a test are representative of the universe. For example, items included in a test may bear superficial similarity to those in the domain of interest, and yet they may require skills that differ from those in the job performance universe. On the other hand, superficial dissimilarity between test and universe does not necessarily constitute evidence against a claim of validity. Methods classed in the content-related category thus should often be concerned with the psychological construct underlying the test as well as with the character of test content. There is often no sharp distinction between test content and test construct.

Content-related evidence of validity is a central concern during test development, whether such development occurs in a research setting, in a publishing house, or in the context of professional practice. Expert professional judgment should play an integral part in developing the definition of what is to be measured, such as describing the universe of content, generating or selecting the content sample, and specifying the item format and scoring system. Thus, inferences about content are linked to test construction as well as to establishing evidence of validity after a test has been developed and chosen for use.

Criterion-Related Evidence

Criterion-related evidence demonstrates that test scores are systematically related to one or more outcome criteria. In this context the criterion is the variable of primary interest, as is determined by a school system, the management of a firm, or clients, for example. The choice of the criterion and the measurement procedures used to obtain criterion scores are of central importance. Logically, the value of a criterion-related study depends on the relevance of the criterion measure that is used.

The relationships between test scores and criterion measures may be expressed in various ways, but the fundamental question is always: "How accurately can criterion performance be predicted from scores on the test?" Whether a given degree of accuracy is judged to be high or low or useful or not useful depends on the context in which the decision is to be made.

Two designs for obtaining criterion-related evidence--predictive and concurrent--can be distinguished. A predictive study obtains information about the accuracy with which early test data can be used to estimate criterion scores that will be obtained in the future. A concurrent study serves the same purpose, but it obtains prediction and criterion information simultaneously. Predictive studies are frequently, but not always, preferable to concurrent studies of selection tests for education or employment, whereas concurrent evidence is usually preferable for achievement tests, tests used for certification, diagnostic clinical tests, or for tests used as measures of a specified construct.

A decision theory framework can be used to judge the value or utility of a predictor test. One judgment can be that the most important error to avoid is a *false positive*--selecting someone who will subsequently fail. Another judgment focuses on avoiding a *false negative*--not selecting people who would have succeeded. The relative cost assigned to each kind of error is again a value judgment; depending on that judgment, the subsequent interpretation of the utility of testing may differ. Value judgments are always involved in selection decisions, if only implicitly. The question of what value judgments are appropriate in individual applications is not addressed in the *Standards*. Questions of utility are relevant to all testing applications.

In contrast to selection decisions, classification decisions attempt to allocate individuals within an institution according to a particular outcome criterion in a way that is optimal for the institution and for the individuals. Test validation for classification decisions requires demonstrating statistical interaction between the test variables and the classification variables. The evidence required depends upon the test application. Careful attention should be paid to the decision that is being made, the criterion used, and the various classifications used.

Validity Generalization

In the past, judgments about the generalization of validity were often based upon nonquantitative reviews of the literature. In more recent years, quantitative meta-analytic techniques have been used frequently to study validity generalization. Both approaches have been used to support inferences about the degree to which validities generalize. Two uses of the results of validity generalization studies may also be distinguished: (a) to draw scientific conclusions and (b) to use the results of validity evidence obtained from prior studies to support the use of a test in a new situation. The latter use raises questions about the degree to which validities are transportable to a specific new situation.

An important issue in educational and employment settings is the degree to which criterion-related evidence of validity that is obtained in one situation can be generalized (that is, transported and used) to another situation without further study of validity in the new situation. If generalization is limited, then local criterion-related evidence of validity may be necessary in most situations in which a test is used. If generalization is extensive, then situation-specific evidence of validity may not be required.

In conducting studies of the generalizability of validity evidence, the prior studies that are included may vary according to several situational facets. Some of the major facets are (a) differences in the way the predictor construct is measured, (b) the type of job or curriculum involved, (c) the type of criterion measure, (d) the type of test takers, and (e) the time period in which the study was conducted. In any particular study of validity generalization, any number of these facets might vary, and a major objective of the study is to determine whether variation in these facets affects the generalizability of validity evidence.

The extent to which predictive or concurrent evidence of validity generalization can be used as criterion-related evidence in new situations is in large measure a function of accumulated research. Consequently, although evidence of generalization can often be used to support a claim of validity in a new situation, the extent to which this claim is justified is constrained by the available data.

Differential Prediction

Differential prediction is a broad concept that includes the possibility that different prediction equations may be obtained for different demographic groups, for groups that differ in their prior experiences, or for groups that receive different treatments or are involved in different instructional programs. The term "treatment" is intended to include not only the various forms of intervention, but also the manner in which tests are administered, such as by computer. The question of the existence of differential prediction is particular to each of these broad categories and to the specific groups within a broad category. For example, there might be differential prediction among groups involved in different instructional programs, but not between groups of black and white students.

In a study of differential prediction among groups that differ in their demographics, prior experiences, or treatments, evidence is needed in order to judge whether a particular test use yields different predictions among those groups (e.g., different predictions for males and females). There is differential prediction, and there may be selection bias, if different algorithms (e.g., regression lines) are derived for different groups and if the predictions lead to decisions regarding people from the individual groups that are systematically different from those decisions obtained from the algorithm based on the pooled groups.

The accepted technical definition of predictive bias implies that no bias exists if the predictive relationship of two groups being compared can be adequately described by a common algorithm (e.g., regression line). In the simple regression analysis for selection using one predictor, selection bias is investigated by judging whether the regressions differ among identifiable groups in the population. If different regression slopes, intercepts, or standard errors of estimate are found among different groups, selection decisions will be biased when the same interpretation is made of a given score without regard to the group from which a person comes. Differing regression slopes or intercepts are taken to indicate that a test is differentially predictive for the groups at hand.

Under these circumstances, a given predictor score yields different criterion predictions for people in different groups and a given criterion score yields a different predictor cut score for people in different groups. If fitting the common prediction equation for the two groups combined suggests that the criterion performance of people in either group is systematically overpredicted or underpredicted, one possibility is to generate a separate algorithm (e.g., regression) for each group. Another possibility is to seek predictor variables that reduce differential prediction without reducing substantially overall predictive accuracy. If separate regressions are considered, the effect of this decision on the distributions of predicted criterion measures for the two groups is usually of interest.

Several proposed ways of evaluating selection bias rest on different definitions of the fairness of a selection procedure. Unlike selection bias, however, fairness is not a technical psychometric term; it is subject to different definitions in different social and political circumstances. At present a consensus of technical experts supports only one approach to selection bias as technically appropriate. This approach is adopted in the *Standards* with the understanding that it does not resolve the larger issue of fairness.

A quite different usage of the term differential prediction arises in the context of placement or classification. In that context evidence is needed to judge the suitability of using a test for classifying or assigning a person to one job versus another or to one treatment versus another. It is possible for tests to be highly predictive of performance for different education programs or jobs without providing the information necessary to make a comparative judgment of the efficacy of assignment or treatment.

Standard 1.1

Evidence of validity should be presented for the major types of inferences for which the use of a test is recommended. A rationale should be provided to support the particular mix of evidence presented for the intended uses. *(Primary)*

Comment:
Whether one or more kinds of validity evidence are appropriate is a function of the particular question being asked and of the context and extent of previous evidence.

Standard 1.2

If validity for some common interpretation has not been investigated, that fact should be made clear, and potential users should be cautioned about making such interpretations. Statements about validity should refer to the validity of particular interpretations or of particular types of decisions. *(Primary)*

Comment:
It is incorrect to use the unqualified phrase "the validity of the test." No test is valid for all purposes or in all situations. If a test is likely to be used incorrectly for certain kinds of decisions, specific warnings against such use should be given. On the other hand, no two situations are ever identical, so some generalization by the user is always necessary. Test developers should present their validation evidence in a way that can aid such generalization.

Standard 1.3	Whenever interpretation of subscores, score differences, or profiles is suggested, the evidence justifying such interpretation should be made explicit. Where composite scores are developed, the basis and rationale for weighting the subscores should be given. *(Primary)*

Comment:
The presented evidence should support the validity of the subscore, or the difference, profile, or other combination score actually used. Evidence based on the total scores is insufficient. A criterion central to the definition of learning disability, for example, is a severe discrepancy between a test taker's performance on a general school ability test and on subject matter achievement tests. Such differences should be found substantially more often in known learning disabled test takers than in other test takers before such differences can be taken as indicative of a learning disability.

Standard 1.4	Whenever it is suggested that the user consider an individual's responses to specific items as a basis for assessment, the test manual should either present evidence supporting this use or call attention to the absence of such evidence. *(Primary)*

Comment:
Users should be warned that inferences that are based on responses to single items are subject to considerable error. Hence, such inferences should be used only to generate hypotheses about a test taker that will be subject to further inquiry.

Standard 1.5	The composition of the validation sample should be described in as much detail as is practicable. Available data on selective factors that might reasonably be expected to influence validity should be described. *(Conditional)*

Comment:
If the subjects of a validity study are patients, for example, the diagnoses of the patients should usually be reported and the severity of the diagnosed condition stated when feasible. For tests used in industry, the employment status (e.g., of applicants and of current job holders), the general level of experience, and the gender composition of the sample should be reported. For tests used in educational settings, relevant information may include community characteristics or selection policies as well as the gender and ethnic composition of the sample.

Standard 1.6	When content-related evidence serves as a significant demonstration of validity for a particular test use, a clear definition of the universe represented, its relevance to the proposed test use, and the procedures followed in generating test content to represent that universe should be described. When the content sampling is intended to reflect criticality rather than representativeness, the rationale for the relative emphasis given to critical factors in the universe should also be described carefully. *(Primary)*

Standard 1.7	When subject-matter experts have been asked to judge whether items are an appropriate sample of a universe or are correctly scored, or when criteria are composed of rater judgments, the relevant training, experience, and qualifications of the experts should be described. Any procedure used to obtain a consensus among judges about the appropriate specifications of the universe and the representativeness of the samples for the intended objectives should also be described. *(Conditional)*

Standard 1.8	When a test is proposed as a measure of a construct, that construct should be distinguished from other constructs; the proposed interpretation of the test score should be explicitly stated; and construct-related evidence should be presented to support such inferences. In particular, evidence should be presented to show that a test does not depend heavily on extraneous constructs. *(Primary)*

Comment:
If a test is intended as a measure of the construct of anxiety, for example, the formulation of the construct should be distinguished from other meanings of the term and should relate the theory in question to that underlying other measures of anxiety discussed in the literature. As another example, some tests, particularly computerized adaptive tests, should be examined to determine whether the same construct is measured in different score ranges. Similarly, the construct measured by speeded tests may change when test format is changed, for example, from paper and pencil to computer.

Standard 1.9	When a test is proposed as a measure of a construct, evidence should be presented to show that the score is more closely related to that construct when it is measured by different methods than it is to substantially different constructs. Furthermore, when several scores are obtained from a single test, each purporting to measure a distinct construct, the intercorrelations among the scores for one or more samples should be reported. *(Secondary)*

Comment:
Relationships among test scores provide important information regarding the distinctiveness of the constructs being measured.

Standard 1.10	Construct-related evidence of validity should demonstrate that the test scores are more closely associated with variables of theoretical interest than they are with variables not included in the theoretical network. *(Conditional)*

Comment:
In some cases the construct purportedly measured by a test is one that is hypothesized to result in score differences among groups with different demographic characteristics (e.g., age, gender, socioeconomic status, and ethnic background). In such cases, evidence of the hypothesized relations between scores and demographics aids score interpretation. In other cases the association of scores with some demographic variables is an indication that a construct other than that purportedly measured by the test may account for score differences. In such cases the test developer should present evidence that the claimed interpretation is warranted among groups that are homogeneous with respect to the demographic

variable in question and should limit interpretation to groups for which validity is demonstrated.

Standard 1.11	**A report of a criterion-related validation study should provide a description of the sample and the statistical analysis used to determine the degree of predictive accuracy. Basic statistics should include numbers of cases (and the reasons for eliminating any cases), measures of central tendency and variability, relationships, and a description of any marked tendency toward nonnormality of distribution.** *(Primary)*

Standard 1.12	**All criterion measures should be described accurately, and the rationale for choosing them as relevant criteria should be made explicit.** *(Primary)*

Comment:
In the case of interest measures, for example, it is sometimes unclear whether the criterion indicates satisfaction, success, or continuance in the activity under examination. When appropriate, attention should be drawn to significant aspects of performance that the criterion measure does not reflect.

Standard 1.13	**The technical quality of all criteria should be considered carefully. Criteria should be determined independently of predictor test scores. If evidence indicates that a criterion measure is affected to a substantial degree by irrelevant factors, this evidence should be reported. If special steps are taken to reduce the effects of irrelevant factors, these steps should be described in detail.** *(Primary)*

Standard 1.14	**When criteria are composed of rater judgments, the degree of knowledge that raters have concerning ratee performance should be reported. If possible, the training and experience of the raters should be described.** *(Primary)*

Standard 1.15	**If more than one criterion measure is obtained, but, for purposes of a particular study, a single composite criterion score is used, the rules for criterion combination should be described.** *(Primary)*

Standard 1.16	**When adequate local validation evidence is not available, criterion-related evidence of validity for a specified test use may be based on validity generalization from a set of prior studies, provided that the specified test-use situation can be considered to have been drawn from the same population of situations on which validity generalization was conducted.** *(Primary)*

Comment:
Several methods of validity generalization and simultaneous estimation have proven useful. In all methods, the integrity of the inference depends on the degree of similarity between the local situation and the prior set

of situations. Present and prior situations can be judged to be similar, for example, according to factors such as the characteristics of the people and job functions involved. Relational measures (correlations, regressions, success rates, etc.) should be carefully selected to be appropriate for the inference to be made.

Standard 1.17	**When statistical adjustments, such as those for restriction of range or attenuation, are made, both adjusted and unadjusted coefficients and all statistics used in the adjustment should be reported.** *(Primary)*

Standard 1.18	**The amount of time that elapses between test administration and collection of criterion data should be reported. Validation reports should be dated clearly and should specify the time interval in which the data were collected.** *(Primary)*

Standard 1.19	**When criterion-related evidence is presented, a rationale for choosing between a predictive and a concurrent design should be available.** *(Conditional)*

Standard 1.20	**Investigations of criterion-related validity for tests used in selection decisions should include, where feasible, a study of the magnitude of predictive bias due to differential prediction for those groups for which previous research has established a substantial prior probability of differential prediction for the particular kind of test in question.** *(Conditional)*

Standard 1.21	**When studies of differential prediction are conducted, the reports should include regression equations (or an appropriate equivalent) computed separately for each group, job, or treatment under consideration or an analysis in which the group, job, or treatment variables are entered as moderators.** *(Primary)* Comment: Correlation coefficients provide inadequate evidence for or against a differential prediction hypothesis if groups, jobs, or treatments are found not to be approximately equal with respect to both test and criterion variances.

Standard 1.22	**To the extent that it is feasible, comparisons of regression equations in studies of differential prediction among groups, jobs, or treatments should include all of the explicit variables that are used in making selection or classification decisions.** *(Secondary)* Comment: Low test reliability or failure to include some variables can result in artifactual differences between regressions for two groups or treatments.

For example, if college admission decisions are made on the basis of a combination of high school rank and selection test scores, but the differential prediction study compares regression of college grades on test scores alone, then a finding of the presence or absence of differential prediction for different applicant groups can result simply from the failure to include both predictors in the regression equations. It should be noted that when such artifactual differences exist, it is the higher scoring group that is more likely to be underpredicted by a particular test.

Standard 1.23 When a test is designed or used to classify people into specified alternative treatment groups (such as alternative occupational, therapeutic, or educational programs) that are typically compared on a common criterion, evidence of the test's differential prediction for this purpose should be provided. *(Secondary)*

Standard 1.24 If specific cut scores are recommended for decision making (for example, in differential diagnosis), the user's guide should caution that the rates of misclassification will vary depending on the percentage of individuals tested who actually belong in each category. *(Primary)*

Comment:
This problem occurs because a decision involves making a judgment about classification or diagnosis given a particular test result, whereas tests are validated by observing the distribution of scores within each category. For example, equal numbers of brain-damaged and psychiatric patients may have been studied during test development, but only a small proportion of brain-damaged people may be found in a psychiatric facility.

Standard 1.25 When a small number of predictors is selected from a large pool and weights are simultaneously determined, the analytic method for selecting variables and weights and for estimating validity coefficients should take into account the bias in the weights and validity coefficients; otherwise the weights and validity coefficients should be cross-validated. *(Primary)*

2. Reliability and Errors of Measurement

Reliability refers to the degree to which test scores are free from errors of measurement. A test taker may perform differently on one occasion than on another for reasons that may or may not be related to the purpose of measurement. A person may try harder, be more fatigued or anxious, have greater familiarity with the content of questions on one test form than another, or simply guess correctly on more questions on one occasion than on another. For these and other reasons, a person's score will not be perfectly consistent from one occasion to the next. Indeed, an individual's scores will rarely be the same on two forms of a test that are intended to be interchangeable. Even the most careful matching of item content and difficulty on two forms of a test cannot ensure that an individual who knows the answer to a particular question on Form A will know the answer to a matched counterpart on Form B.

Differences between scores from one form to another or from one occasion to another may be attributable to what is commonly called *errors of measurement*. Such differences are not attributable to errors of measurement if maturation, intervention, or some other event has made these differences meaningful or if inconsistency of response is relevant to the construct being measured. Measurement errors reduce the reliability (and therefore the generalizability) of the score obtained for a person from a single measurement. The magnitude of the error notwithstanding, the importance of a particular source of error depends on the specific use of a test.

Fundamental to the proper evaluation of a test are the identification of major sources of measurement error, the size of the errors resulting from these sources, the indication of the degree of reliability to be expected between pairs of scores under particular circumstances, and the generalizability of results across items, forms, raters, administrations, and other measurement facets.

Typically, test developers and publishers have primary responsibility for obtaining and reporting evidence concerning reliability and errors of measurement adequate for the intended uses. The typical user generally will not conduct separate reliability studies. Users do have a responsibility, however, to determine that the available information regarding reliability and errors of measurement is relevant to their intended uses and interpretations and, in the absence of such information, to provide the necessary evidence.

Reliability coefficient is a generic term. Different reliability coefficients and estimates of components of measurement error can be based on various types of evidence; each type of evidence suggests a different meaning. A reliability coefficient based on the relation between alternate forms of a test administered on two separate occasions is affected by several sources of error, including random response variability, changes in the individuals taking the tests, differences in the content of the forms, and differences in administration. On the other hand, analyses of part scores or item scores from a single administration of a test do not give information on response variability because of the latter three sources of error.

It is essential, therefore, that the method used to estimate reliability takes into account those sources of error of greatest concern for a particular use and interpretation of a test. Not all sources of error are expected to be relevant for a given test. Thus the estimation of clearly labeled components of observed and error score variance is a particularly useful outcome of a reliability study, both for the test developer who wishes to improve the reliability of an instrument and for the user who wants to interpret test scores in particular circumstances with maximum understanding. Reporting standard errors, confidence intervals, or other measures of imprecision of estimates is also helpful. Reporting a reliability coefficient alone, which typically varies more from one group of test takers to another, is less informative.

Estimates of the reliability of a test should consider not only the relevant sources of error, but also the types of decisions anticipated to be based on the test scores and on their expected levels of aggregation (individual versus groups of test takers). For example, tests are sometimes used as the primary basis for making dichotomous decisions. In testing to determine certification for successful completion of a course of study, the primary interest is in the decision. Of course, there may be more than two categories, but the pass-fail or mastery-nonmastery decision is common. Estimates of the consistency of decisions are needed whenever decision rules assign people to categories according to specified test score intervals. An estimate of the standard error of measurement at the cut score is helpful.

Standard 2.1

For each total score, subscore, or combination of scores that is reported, estimates of relevant reliabilities and standard errors of measurement should be provided in adequate detail to enable the test user to judge whether scores are sufficiently accurate for the intended use of the test. *(Primary)*

Comment:
It is not sufficient to report estimates of reliabilities and standard errors of measurement for only total scores when subscores are also reported. The form-to-form consistency of total scores on an achievement test may be acceptably high, for example, yet content specific subscores may still show relatively poor form-to-form consistency. When subscores are reported, users need information about their reliabilities and standard errors of measurement.

Composite scores may take various forms, some of which may be expected to be more reliable than the parts and some less reliable than the parts. But scores representing differences between scores obtained from two tests or from repeated administrations of the same test (called *gain scores*) are generally less reliable than either of the parts. Scholastic ability tests are often used to predict achievement test scores, and the difference (or residual score) is computed between the observed score and the predicted score. Such residual scores are, in general, less reliable than the original observed scores. Another composite score that is usually less reliable than are its parts is a ratio score.

Standard 2.2

The procedures that are used to obtain samples of individuals, groups, or observations for the purpose of estimating reliabilities and standard errors of measurement, as well as the nature of the populations involved, should be described. The numbers of individuals in each sample that are used to obtain the estimates, score means, and standard deviations should also be reported. *(Primary)*

Standard 2.3

Each method of estimating a reliability that is reported should be defined clearly and expressed in terms of variance components, correlation coefficients, standard errors of measurement, percentages of correct decisions, or equivalent statistics. The conditions under which the reliability estimate was obtained and the situations to which it may be applicable should also be explained clearly. *(Primary)*

Comment:
Because there are many ways of estimating reliability, each influenced by different sources of measurement error, it is unacceptable to say simply, "The reliability of test X is .90." A better statement is, "Based on the correlation between alternate test forms A and C administered on successive days to a sample of 100 tenth-grade students from a middle-class suburban public school in New York, the alternate form reliability is estimated to be .90, with an approximate 95% confidence interval of (.85-.93)."

Standard 2.4

If reliability coefficients are adjusted for restriction of range, both the adjusted and unadjusted coefficients should be reported together with the standard deviations of the group actually tested and of the group for which adjusted estimates are presented. *(Primary)*

Standard 2.5

Estimates of reliability that are based on alternate forms of a test administered to the same sample of individuals on two separate occasions should indicate the order in which forms were administered, the interval between administrations, and a rationale for choosing that interval. Means and standard deviations obtained from both forms should be provided, as well as standard errors of measurement and the estimate of the alternate-form reliability. *(Primary)*

Comment:
An observed score typically represents the performance of a test taker during a particular period of time, which may be a few years, several months, or only an hour or so (as in measures of mood, for example). Evidence should be provided for the consistency of the information obtained by independent measurements on two or more occasions during the period in which test interpreters are likely to regard a person's score as stable.

In some cases it may be advisable to obtain scores on more than two occasions, particularly if considerable instability is expected. Where parallel forms are used in an investigation of stability, it should be recognized that content differences between forms, as well as instability, contribute to the error variance. Estimates of stability based on a retest with the same form, however, may be spuriously inflated due to the effects of memory.

Standard 2.6

Coefficients based on internal analysis should not be interpreted as substitutes for alternate-form reliability or estimates of stability over time unless other evidence supports that interpretation in a particular context. *(Primary)*

Standard 2.7

Procedures known to yield inflated estimates of reliability for speeded tests should not be used to estimate the reliability of a highly speeded test. *(Primary)*

Comment:
For example, split-half coefficients that are obtained from scoring odd and even numbered test items separately yield an inflated estimate for a highly speeded test and are thus inappropriate.

Standard 2.8   Where judgmental processes enter into the scoring of a test, evidence on the degree of agreement between independent scorings should be provided. If such evidence has not yet been provided, attention should be drawn to scoring variations as a possible significant source of errors of measurements. *(Primary)*

Comment:
Variance component analyses are especially helpful for judgmentally scored tests; these analyses provide separate variance estimates for questions, judges, scales used in the rating process, and time allowance, for example. Inter-rater or inter-observer agreement may be particularly important when observational data that involve subtle discriminations are collected.

Standard 2.9   Where there are generally accepted theoretical or empirical reasons for expecting that reliabilities or standard errors of measurement differ substantially for different populations, estimates should be presented for each major population for which the test is recommended. *(Conditional)*

Comment:
The reliability obtained for a general population is of limited value to a test user who is working with a restricted population. For example, a user working with only speech-impaired individuals would be better informed by stability coefficients and standard errors of measurement based on a sample of speech-impaired persons than by those based on a general population. Similarly, a reliability coefficient based on a sample of students spanning several grades would generally give a highly inflated estimate of reliability for that test administered in a single grade. In this case, it is better to report reliabilities and standard errors of measurement separately for each grade level.

Standard 2.10   Standard errors of measurement should be reported at critical score levels. Where cut scores are specified for selection or classification, the standard errors of measurement should be reported for score levels at or near the cut score. *(Secondary)*

Comment:
Reporting standard errors of measurement at every score level may not be feasible in some circumstances, but they should be reported at appropriate, well-separated levels or intervals.

Standard 2.11   In adaptive testing, estimates of the magnitude of errors of measurement, based on the analysis of the results from repeated administrations using different items, should be provided. *(Secondary)*

Comment:
Although estimates of standard errors of measurement may be computed and reported routinely as part of the adaptive testing procedure, those estimates are not a substitute for estimates based on paired administrations of the adaptive test. The former estimates assume the adequacy of both the item parameter estimates and the item response theory. Estimates of reliabilities and standard errors of measurement based on the administration and analysis of alternate forms of the

adaptive test do not require these assumptions. Hence, the alternate form estimates provide an independent check on the magnitude of the errors of measurement in adaptive testing.

In some situations the results of traditional paper-and-pencil tests for some test takers may be reported and used concurrently with the results of computerized adaptive tests administered to other test takers. In such situations, the paper-and-pencil and the computerized adaptive tests should not be treated automatically as alternate forms. Estimates of means and methods variance should be obtained by administering and analyzing the test by both methods, using an appropriate sample of test takers. If methods variance is small, the tests can be considered parallel.

Standard 2.12   **For dichotomous decisions, estimates should be provided of the percentage of test takers who are classified in the same way on two occasions or on alternate forms of the test.** *(Conditional)*

3. Test Development and Revision

Background

This chapter covers issues of general concern to test developers, emphasizing how test development research can provide the basis for examining issues discussed in other chapters. Test developers have a responsibility to provide evidence regarding reliability and validity for stated testing purposes, as well as manuals and norms, when appropriate, to guide proper interpretation. They also need to anticipate how their tests will be used and misused, to do research that helps distinguish proper from improper uses, and to design tests and accompanying materials in ways that promote proper uses. The mode of presentation, that is, manuals or other materials, is not specified in many of the following standards; however, the test developer, publisher, or sponsor has a responsibility to present information in a readily available form, with summaries and interpretations, to facilitate test review and evaluation.

Although it is concerned with strengthening current testing practices, the *Standards* is also intended to encourage the development of new and improved tests, so that the contributions of tests and testing to society can be extended. Advances in testing stem from research in a variety of areas. For example, some experiments in cognitive psychology are being transformed into faceted diagnostic assessment batteries; physiological and neuropsychological measures are being investigated as potential selection and classification devices; learning sample tests and learning style inventories are being used to prescribe educational treatments; and computerized adaptive and interactive testing, multimedia test presentations, and computerized interpretations are being used increasingly. In the *Standards* an attempt is made to anticipate problems posed by such developments and to facilitate advantages they offer.

The standards in this chapter cover test and item specifications, item analysis and selection procedures, and the evaluation of test designs for intended uses. Some special standards applicable to particular types of tests, including computerized tests, are also included.

Standard 3.1

Tests and testing programs should be developed on a sound scientific basis. Test developers should compile the evidence bearing on a test, decide which information is needed prior to test publication or distribution and which information can be provided later, and conduct any needed research. *(Primary)*

Standard 3.2

The specifications used in constructing items or selecting observations and in designing the test instrument as a whole should be stated clearly. The definition of a universe or domain that is used for constructing or selecting items should be described. When, for reasons of security, sample copies of a test are unavailable for inspection, the descriptive information should include a representative item identified with each major cell in the classification or domain definition. When item difficulty is a facet of such a system, items representative of the difficulty levels should be provided. *(Conditional)*

Comment:
Test specifications sometimes indicate that a test is criterion-referenced as opposed to norm-referenced, and this practice has led to some confusion. In norm-referenced interpretations, a score (for an individual or for a definable group) is compared with distributions of scores for other

individuals or groups. In criterion-referenced interpretations, the score is taken to reflect directly a level of competence in some defined criterion domain. Although tests built with different reference specifications may differ in various ways, the interpretation of the test scores--not the test itself--is norm-referenced or criterion-referenced. Thus some norm-referenced tests can be interpreted in criterion-referenced ways and vice versa.

The adequacy and usefulness of criterion-referenced interpretations depend on the rigor with which the behavioral domain represented by the test has been defined. Such interpretations are intended to describe the status of individuals or groups with respect to one or more behavioral domains, and it is the domain definition that provides the primary reference for interpretation of scores and for judging the adequacy of the test. The domain definition should be sufficiently detailed and delimiting to show clearly what facets of behavior are included and what facets are excluded in the domain. Within the domain, the classification system adopted should show clearly what and how many facets of behavior the domain comprises.

Standard 3.3

Domain definitions and the test specifications should be sufficiently clear so that knowledgeable experts can judge the relations of items to the domains they represent. *(Primary)*

Standard 3.4

When test items relate to a course of training or study, a curriculum, a textbook, or packaged instruction, the manual or other reports should include an identification and description of the course or instructional materials and should indicate the year in which these materials were prepared. *(Secondary)*

Standard 3.5

When selecting the type and content of items for tests and inventories, test developers should consider the content and type in relation to cultural backgrounds and prior experiences of the variety of ethnic, cultural, age, and gender groups represented in the intended population of test takers. *(Conditional)*

Comment:
For some kinds of test content, cultural background factors are irrelevant, as in simple numerical tests of arithmetic skills or in some employment tests. When the relevance of such factors is in doubt, test developers might establish a review process using expert judges both to select item material and to eliminate material likely to be inappropriate or offensive for groups in the test-taking population. Logical exceptions to this standard are tests of English designed for and used with diverse foreign populations and tests of foreign languages for English-speaking populations.

At various points in test development, empirical procedures may be needed. Such procedures may be needed, for example, when constructing interest inventories, in which differential item response rates may exist for different gender, ethnic, and educational groups. Differential response rates do not necessarily invalidate such items or scales based on them. However, the developer's aim should be to maximize scale validity and, within this constraint, the developer should strive to minimize the potential misrepresentation of interests for major groups in the population that is served.

Standard 3.6   In the development of occupational interest inventories, where a wide range of duties and activities is subsumed under a given occupational title, the extent to which average patterns of interests or abilities for an occupation are compatible with the major specialties within that occupation should be reported to the users. *(Secondary)*

Standard 3.7   When correlations of item scores with criterion scores that are external to the test in question are used to select items or construct scoring keys, item validities should be accompanied by evidence of cross-validation for the scale. *(Secondary)*

Standard 3.8   When parameter estimates of item response curves are used in test development, the item response model and calibration procedures should be specified clearly. Information about the degree to which important item response theory assumptions (e.g., unidimensionality or equality of slope parameters) are satisfied should be presented in order to demonstrate the adequacy of the fit of the model to the data. The sample used for estimating item parameters should be described and should be of adequate size and diversity for the estimation procedure. *(Conditional)*

Comment:
Although overall sample size is important, it is important also that there be an adequate number of cases in regions critical to the determination of item parameters.

Standard 3.9   For adaptive tests, the rationale and supporting evidence for procedures used in selecting items for administration, in stopping the test, and in scoring the test should be described in the test manual. *(Primary)*

Standard 3.10   When previous research indicates the need for studies of item or test performance differences for a particular kind of test for members of age, ethnic, cultural, and gender groups in the population of test takers, such studies should be conducted as soon as is feasible. Such research should be designed to detect and eliminate aspects of test design, content, or format that might bias test scores for particular groups. *(Conditional)*

Comment:
Although it may not have been possible prior to first release of a test to study the question of differential performance and item bias for some groups, continued operational use of a test will often afford opportunities to check for group differences in test performance and to investigate whether or not these differences indicate test bias.

Standard 3.11   When test-taking strategies that are unrelated to the constructs or content being measured have been found to influence test performance significantly, these strategies should be explained to test takers before the test is administered either in an information booklet or, if the explanation can be made briefly, along with the test directions. The use of such strategies by all test takers should be encouraged if their effect facilitates performance and discouraged if their effect interferes with performance. *(Primary)*

Comment:
Test-taking strategies, such as guessing, skipping all doubtful items, or skipping and then returning to doubtful items as time allows, can influence test scores positively or negatively depending on the scoring system used and aspects of item and test design such as speededness or the number of response alternatives provided in multiple-choice items. Differential use of such strategies by test takers can result in reduced test reliability and validity. The goal of test directions, therefore, should be to convey information on the possible effectiveness of various strategies and thus provide all test takers an equal opportunity to perform optimally.

Standard 3.12 Probable sources of variance that would confound the construct or domain definitions underlying the test should be investigated by the test developer, and the implications of the results for test design, interpretation, and use should be presented in the technical manual or in supplementary reports. In general, evidence from research should be provided to justify the use of novel item or test formats. *(Secondary)*

Standard 3.13 For tests that impose strict time limits, test development research should examine the degree to which scores include a speed component and evaluate the appropriateness of that component, given the constructs or content the test is designed to measure. *(Conditional)*

Standard 3.14 The sensitivity of test performance to improvement with practice, coaching, or brief instruction should be studied as part of developmental research, especially on performance tests that use an unfamiliar response mode, such as computer-administered tests. A test that is designed to measure learning from practice, coaching, or instruction should be shown to do so, and a test that is designed to be unaffected by these forms of learning should be shown to be so. Materials to aid in score interpretation should summarize evidence derived from such studies to indicate the degree to which improvement with practice or coaching can be expected. *(Secondary)*

Standard 3.15 For interest or personality measures intended for selection or placement purposes, evidence should be presented on the extent to which scores are susceptible to an attempt by test takers to present false or unduly favorable pictures of themselves. *(Secondary)*

Standard 3.16 The score report forms and instructional materials for a test, including computerized reports and materials, should facilitate appropriate interpretations. *(Primary)*

Comment:
This standard is particularly important in the case of computer programs or computerized reports provided to test takers.

Standard 3.17

If a short form of a test is prepared by reducing the number of items or organizing portions of a test into a separate form, empirical data or a theoretical rationale should be provided to estimate the reliability of each short form and its correlation with the standard form. *(Primary)*

Standard 3.18

A test should be amended or revised when new research data, significant changes in the domain represented, or new conditions of test use and interpretation make the test inappropriate for its intended uses. An apparently old test that remains useful need not be withdrawn or revised simply because of the passage of time. But it is the responsibility of test developers and test publishers to monitor changing conditions and to amend, revise, or withdraw the test as indicated. *(Primary)*

Standard 3.19

Tests should not be titled or advertised as "revised" unless they have been revised in significant ways. A phrase such as "with minor modification" should be used when the test has been modified in minor ways. The score scale should be adjusted to account for these modifications. *(Primary)*

Standard 3.20

If a test or part of a test is intended for research use only and is not distributed for operational use, this fact should be displayed prominently in any materials provided for interpreting individual scores. *(Primary)*

Standard 3.21

The directions for test administration should be presented with sufficient clarity and emphasis so that it is possible to approximate for others the administrative conditions under which the norms and the data on reliability and validity were obtained. *(Primary)*

Comment:
Because people administering tests in schools, industry, and in other settings sometimes may not understand the need to follow instructions closely, it is necessary that test administrators receive detailed and insistent instruction on this point.

Standard 3.22

The directions presented to a test taker should be detailed enough so that test takers can respond to a task in the manner that the test developer intends. When appropriate, sample material and practice or sample questions should be provided. *(Primary)*

Comment:
For example, in a personality inventory it may be intended that test takers give the first response that occurs to them. Such an expectation

should be made clear in the inventory directions. In directions for interest inventories, it may be important to specify whether test takers are to mark the activities they would like ideally or whether they are to consider both the opportunity and ability realistically.

The extent and nature of practice material depends on expected levels of knowledge among test takers. It may, for example, be very important to provide practice before a novel test format is administered. When appropriate, the directions should describe clearly such matters as guessing and time limits.

If expansion or elaboration of the test instructions is permitted, the conditions under which this may be done should be stated clearly either in the form of general rules or by giving representative examples, or both. If no expansion or elaboration is to be permitted, this should be stated explicitly. Publishers should include guidance for dealing with typical questions from test takers.

Standard 3.23

When structured behavior samples are collected within a standardized testing format, the specific type of behavior expected should be defined clearly. Directions to a test taker that are intended to produce a particular behavior sample (often called a "prompt") should be standardized, just as the directions are standardized for any other test. Test instructions should be pretested. *(Conditional)*

Comment:
In framing a prompt, the age and ability level of test takers should be considered, as should other possible unique sources of difficulty for groups in the population to be tested. In particular, directions that specify time allowances, minimum lengths of the samples expected, and rules regarding use of supplementary materials (such as notes, references, calculators, or dictionaries) should be pretested.

Standard 3.24

Procedures for scoring tests locally should be presented by the test developer in sufficient detail and clarity to maximize the accuracy of scoring. Instructions for rating scales or for scores obtained by coding, scaling, or classifying free responses should define each scale clearly. *(Primary)*

Standard 3.25

Where judgments enter into test scoring, the bases for scoring and the procedures for training scorers should be presented by the developer in sufficient detail to permit a level of agreement among scorers comparable to that under which the norms were generated. When appropriate, attention should be drawn to scoring variations as a possible significant source of errors of measurement. *(Conditional)*

4. Scaling, Norming, Score Comparability, and Equating

Background

Interpreting test scores can often be aided by the availability of scoring scales and norms that relate raw scores to defined theoretical or empirical distributions. Although the content and construct interpretations of a test are primary, the meaning of a score is often enhanced by the scales and norms to which it can be referenced. When comparing scores from multiple forms, revised forms, or even different tests, meaning is derived from equating scores or adjusting scales to achieve comparability.

Scales and Norms

Because raw test scores are expressed in units that result from arbitrary features of the test, a wide variety of derived scales has been developed for reporting scores for different purposes. The existence of numerous derived scales sometimes results in confusion and misunderstanding. Norms provide a basis for interpreting the test performance of a person or group in relation to a defined population of persons or groups. Many different kinds of norms may be appropriate for a given test use: local norms, based on sampling from the population or specified groups in a particular locality; state or regional norms; norms based on national probability sampling; and norms based on a wide variety of occupational and educational classifications or on institutions such as schools or colleges.

Norms, and particularly national norms, are extremely difficult and costly to construct properly and should not be produced automatically or be required for all published tests. Some tests, for example, have only "user norms" or "program norms" that consist of descriptive statistics based on all test takers in a given period of time rather than norms obtained by formal sampling methods. Although descriptive statistics such as those based on people who happen to take the test are often useful, they should not be confused with norms representative of more precisely identifiable groups.

Comparability and Equating

Multiple forms of a test are required in many testing situations. In an admissions testing program, for example, different forms are used in different administrations so that information about specific items on the test cannot be made available to test takers at a second administration, thereby possibly giving them an unfair advantage over the people who took that test on the first administration. Alternate forms of a test are also needed in many other situations, such as in measuring student learning with achievement tests, and in licensing and certification tests.

Ideally, alternate forms of a test are interchangeable in use. That is, it should be a matter of indifference to anyone taking the test or to anyone using the test results whether form A or form B of the test was used. Of course, such an ideal cannot be attained fully in practice. Even minor variations in content from one form to the next can prevent the forms from being interchangeable since one form may favor individuals with particular strengths, whereas a second form may favor those with slightly different strengths.

If only raw scores were reported, unintended differences in overall test difficulty from form to form would give an advantage to people taking the easier form. Therefore, it is usually necessary to convert the scores obtained on one form to the units of the other, a process commonly called test equating. The conversion may involve either an equation or a table of converted scores associated with each observed score (e.g., the number of right answers on the test form). In either case, the conversion will be subject to error due to the conversion procedure and sampling.

Test forms that differ in reliability cannot be equated in the strict sense. A candidate whose expected test score is below some established cut score is more likely to pass the test, in the sense of obtaining a score above the cut score by choosing the less reliable test and hoping for a favorable measurement error. On the other hand, people who expect scores above the cut score should prefer the more accurate test, to minimize the chance of an unfavorable measurement error.

Despite the fact that tests that differ in reliability cannot be equated in a strict sense, it is often desirable to convert the scores so that they are as comparable as possible in some particular sense. Such conversions are frequently referred to as equating, but the label is misleading. A more appropriate description is that the scores have been scaled to achieve comparability. To say that scores have been made comparable is a weaker claim than to say that they have been equated. Equated scores are meant to be interchangeable, whereas comparable scores are meant to be similar in a particular sense. For example, comparable scores may correspond to the same percentile ranks in a particular population. It would not necessarily follow that persons of equal ability would have the same probability of achieving a given score, nor would it follow that comparable scores would correspond to the same percentile in some other population. Both of these interpretations would follow, however, for scores that are rigorously equated.

Just as it is impossible to equate scores when tests differ in reliability, it is also impossible to equate scores from tests that measure different characteristics. For example, a person with strong verbal and weak mathematical skills is likely to score higher on a verbal test than on a mathematics test where those tests have been scaled such that a given score corresponds to the same percentile rank for a specified population of test takers. Even when different characteristics are being measured, it is often convenient to scale the scores to be comparable in a particular sense for a particular population. There should be no implication, however, that the scores are equated, since equating applies only when the same characteristic is being measured by the tests.

More difficult problems arise when tests measure similar, yet not identical, characteristics. Three common situations serve as examples: (a) equating tests that have similar titles and purposes but that have different content specifications and are produced by different test publishers, (b) equating a new form to an old form following a major revision in the test specifications, and (c) vertically equating tests designed to be most appropriate at different developmental or educational levels (e.g., equating a test designed for grades 2 and 3 with one designed for grades 4 and 5). In each of these cases, there may be good reasons for wanting the scores to be scaled such that they are as comparable as possible in a particular sense. The procedures used to achieve comparability may be the same as those used in test equating, but the strict requirements of test equating will not be satisfied, and, therefore, the resulting scores should be called scaled or comparable rather than equated.

When there are changes in test specifications or when there are substantial differences in forms, it still may be necessary to compare scores from old and new forms of the test. Hence, the scores based on the new form need to be converted in order to be as comparable as possible to those on the old form, despite the fact that they cannot be made strictly equivalent. In fact, the conversion will not be unique but will depend on the definition of comparability, the groups on which the conversion is based, and the method of conversion.

Standard 4.1	Scales used for reporting scores and the rationale for choosing them should be described clearly in test publications to facilitate accurate interpretation of scores by both the test user and the test taker. A publication should specify how scaled scores are derived from raw scores. *(Primary)*

Comment:
All scales (raw score or derived) are subject to misinterpretations. Sometimes scales are extrapolated beyond the range of available data or are interpolated without sufficient data points. Grade- and age-equivalent scores have been criticized heavily in this regard, but percentile ranks and standard score scales are also subject to misinterpretation. Test publishers and users can reduce misinterpretations of grade-equivalent scores, for example, by ensuring that such scores are (a) reported only for grades in which actual growth can be expected, (b) reported only for grades for which test data are available, and (c) accompanied by instructions that make clear that grade-equivalent scores do not represent a standard of growth per year or grade and that 50% of the students tested in the standardization sample should by definition fall below grade level, that if a student scores above grade level it does not necessarily mean that the student has mastered the content material of the higher grade level, and that interpretations of differences between grade equivalent scores on separate subtests should be avoided.

Standard 4.2	When scaled scores are used, the scale chosen should be consistent with the intended purposes of the test and should be described in detail. When raw scores are used, they should be demonstrated to have the same desirable properties as do scaled scores. *(Primary)*

Standard 4.3	Norms that are presented should refer to clearly described groups. These groups should be the ones with whom users of the test will ordinarily wish to compare the people who are tested. Test publishers should also encourage the development of local norms by test users when the published norms are insufficient for particular test users. *(Conditional)*

Comment:
When tests are developed for uses other than local use, the user needs to know the applicability of the test to different groups. Differentiated norms or summary information about differences between gender, ethnic, grade, or age groups, for example, may be useful. Users also need to be made alert to situations in which norms are less appropriate for one group than for another. For example, the manual for an occupational interest inventory should point out that a person who has a high degree of interest in an occupation as compared to people in general may have a lower degree of interest as compared to people actually engaged in that occupation.

Standard 4.4	Reports of norming studies should include the year in which normative data were collected, provide descriptive statistics, and describe the sampling design and participation rates in sufficient detail so that the study can be evaluated for appropriateness. *(Primary)*

Comment:
Test users may say that a test taker's performance is at a particular level, for example, even though the norms are obtained from only schools

that voluntarily participated in the test research. In this instance, norms of the volunteer group of schools cannot be assumed to apply to schools in general.

Standard 4.5   When it is expected that a test will be used to make norm-referenced assessments of groups rather than of individuals, normative data based on appropriate group statistics should be provided. *(Secondary)*

Standard 4.6   When scores earned on different forms of a test, including computer-presented or computerized adaptive tests, are intended to be used interchangeably, data concerning the parallelism of the forms should be available. Details of the equivalence study should be available, including specific information about the method of equating: the administrative design and statistical procedures used, the characteristics of the anchor test, if any, and of the sampling procedures; information on the sample; and sample size. Periodic checks on the adequacy of the equating should be reported. *(Primary)*

Standard 4.7   Content specifications that are changed from an earlier version of a test to a later version should be identified in the test manual, and an indication should be given that converted scores may not be strictly equivalent. In addition, when radical shifts in test specifications occur, either a new scale should be introduced or a clear statement should be provided with the scores to alert users that the scores are not interchangeable with those on earlier versions of the test. *(Conditional)*

Comment:
Major shifts sometimes occur in the content specifications of tests that are used for substantial periods of time. Often such changes take advantage of improvements in item types or of shifts in content that have been shown to improve validity and, therefore, are highly desirable. It is important to recognize, however, that such shifts will result in scores that cannot be made strictly interchangeable with scores on an earlier form of the test. Nonetheless, it is often useful to report scores that are as comparable as possible.

Standard 4.8   When an anchor test design is used in equating test forms, the characteristics of the anchor test should be described, particularly in its relation to the forms being equated. Content specifications for the anchor test and statistical information regarding the relationships between the anchor test and each form should be provided separately for the sample of people taking each form. *(Secondary)*

Comment:
Although an anchor test may be used to improve the precision of the equating, its primary purpose is to adjust for possible differences (e.g., ability level) in the groups taking different forms. It is important to have information regarding the magnitude of those differences on the anchor test.

Standard 4.9   Continuing testing programs that attempt to maintain a common scale over time should conduct periodic checks of the stability of the scale. *(Conditional)*

5. Test Publication: Technical Manuals and User's Guides

Background

Publishers should provide enough information for a qualified user or a reviewer of a test to evaluate the appropriateness and technical adequacy of the test. Separate reference material should be detailed for each mode of presentation of the test, e.g. paper and pencil, computer, etc. Illustrations of interpretation of scores as they relate to the test developer's intended applications should be provided so that the test user may make professional judgement about the inferences he or she wishes to make on the basis of the scores obtained from the tests. Technical data that are required prior to the release of the test for operational use are usually summarized with appropriate references in a *technical manual*. The manual need not normally contain more than summaries of research, but references noted in the manual generally should be readily obtainable by the test user. In many situations the details of the research base can be provided in separate volumes, or when demand is likely to be low they may be maintained only in archival form, including electronic storage.

A manual should be evaluated on the basis of its completeness, accuracy, and clarity. If the typical user of the manual is likely to gain an inaccurate impression, the manual is poorly written. A manual should communicate information to many different groups. Sometimes tests are selected for use by highly qualified people but are actually used by people with minimal training in testing. Such users may not understand technical discussions or detailed statistical information. Other users who are measurement specialists need to be able to judge the technical adequacy of the test on the basis of information in the manual or in its supplements. Separate documents or sections of the manual may be written for identifiable categories of users (e.g., counselors, school psychologists, administrators, teachers, researchers, or test takers). Whatever the form of the manual and its supplements, the prospective test user or those affected by the test use should have the information needed for making necessary judgments about the test or resulting scores. Test developers and publishers should, therefore, provide information in manuals to help reduce the likelihood of misunderstanding or misuse of test scores.

Even when a test (or test battery) is developed for use within a single organization, a brief manual will be useful. Preparation of a manual helps the test developer organize thought, codify procedures, and communicate ideas and intentions to test users and, when appropriate, to external reviewers of tests and testing procedures. Manuals should also be prepared for mandated testing programs--regardless of the source of the mandate.

Many of the other chapters of the *Standards* contain specific standards with implications for test manuals and user's guides. Therefore, those responsible for the preparation of these documents should consult the index entries under test manuals and user's guides to locate other relevant standards. In this chapter more general standards regarding the construction and publication of test manuals are provided.

Standard 5.1

A technical manual should be made available to prospective test users at the time a test is published or released for operational use. *(Conditional)*

Comment:
The test developer or publisher should judge carefully which information should be included in the first edition of the technical manual and which information can be provided in supplements. The determining factors in

35

this decision are the potential volume of test use, the cost of publishing the materials, and the potential impact on test takers and test users resulting from use of the test. For low-volume, unpublished tests, documentation may be presented in a relatively brief statement. When the developer is also the user, necessary documentation and summaries should be available, but a published test manual is not required.

Standard 5.2	Test manuals should describe thoroughly the rationale for the test, state the recommended uses of the test, and provide a summary of the support for such uses. Where particular misuses of a test can be reasonably anticipated, the test manual should provide specific cautions against such misuses. *(Primary)*
Standard 5.3	Technical manuals should cite a balanced and representative set of studies regarding general and specific test uses. The cited studies, except published work, dissertations, and proprietary studies, should be made available on request to the prospective test user by the publisher. *(Conditional)*
Standard 5.4	Test manuals should identify any special qualifications that are required to administer a test and to interpret it properly. Statements of user qualifications should identify the specific training, certification, or experience needed. *(Primary)*
Standard 5.5	Test manuals should be amended, supplemented, or revised as necessary to keep information for users up-to-date and to provide useful, additional information or cautions. *(Conditional)*
Standard 5.6	In addition to publishing test manuals with amendments, supplements, and revisions, test developers and publishers should respond to reasonable requests for additional information, which may be required in order to determine the appropriateness of intended test use. When, in the judgment of the test developer or publisher, a particular test use cannot be justified, the response to an inquiry from a prospective test user should indicate this fact clearly. *(Secondary)*
Standard 5.7	Promotional material for a test should be accurate. Publishers should avoid using advertising techniques that suggest that a test can accomplish more than is supported by its research base. *(Primary)*
Standard 5.8	Statements in a test manual that report relationships between test scores and criteria are by implication quantitative and should be so stated. *(Primary)*

Comment:
A manual might suggest, for example, that spatial ability is required for architecture or engineering. Such a statement is quantitatively inadequate because it does not indicate the degree to which architectural success has been found to depend upon spatial ability.

Standard 5.9

If a test is designed so that more than one method can be used for the recording of responses, such as making responses in a test booklet and on separate answer sheets, then the manual should report data, references, or a logically developed argument on the degree to which results from these methods are interchangeable. If the results are not interchangeable, this fact should be reported, and guidance should be given for the interpretation of scores obtained under the various conditions or methods of administration. *(Primary)*

Standard 5.10

A test manual should not suggest that a test is self-interpreting unless there is evidence supporting the validity of this claim. In the absence of such evidence, a manual should specify information to be given about test results to people who lack the training usually required to interpret them. Tests that are designed to be scored by the test taker should be accompanied by interpretive aids. *(Primary)*

Comment:
The manual for one interest inventory, for example, indicates that test takers may perform the mechanics of scoring their own tests but properly stresses that they need the help of a trained teacher or counselor in interpreting the scores.

Standard 5.11

Organizations offering automated test interpretation should make available information on the rationale of the test and a summary of the evidence supporting the interpretations given. This information should include the validity of the cut scores or configural rules used and a description of the samples from which they were derived. *(Primary)*

Comment:
The release of cut scores or configural rules is a very desirable practice. When proprietary interests result in the withholding of such algorithms, arrangements might be made for an external review of these algorithms under professional auspices, which ensures adequate protection of any proprietary material.

Part II

Professional Standards
for Test Use

6. General Principles of Test Use

Background

Although a distinction is made in the *Standards* between test development and test use, that distinction is not always clear in application. For example, test administration, scoring, and reporting may be done by the test developer or the test user. Also users need to be aware of standards governing test development so that they can more easily evaluate the tests they contemplate using. This chapter contains general standards applicable to test use in professional practice. Succeeding chapters in this section present standards more specific to specialty areas.

In applying standards to test use, as opposed to test development, more flexibility and use of professional judgment are required. The appropriateness of specific test uses cannot be evaluated in the abstract but only in the context of the larger assessment process. The principal questions to be asked in evaluating test use are whether or not the test is appropriate (valid) for its specific role in the larger assessment process and whether or not the test user has accurately described the extent to which the score supports any decision made or administrative action taken.

Although it is not appropriate to tell a test user that particular levels of predictive validity and reliability need to be met, it is appropriate to ask the user to ascertain that procedures result in adequately valid predictions or reliable classifications for the purposes of the testing. Cost-benefit compromises become as necessary in test use as they do in test development. However, as with standards for test development, when test standards are not met in test use, reasons should be available. Here again, the criteria of impact on test takers applies. The greater the potential impact, the greater the need to satisfy relevant standards.

The test user, in selecting or interpreting a test, should know the purposes of the testing and the probable consequences. The user should know the procedures necessary to facilitate effectiveness and to reduce bias in test use. Although the test developer and publisher should provide information on the strengths and weaknesses of the test, the ultimate responsibility for appropriate test use lies with the test user. The user should become knowledgeable about the test and its appropriate uses and also communicate this information, as appropriate, to others.

Standard 6.1

Test users should evaluate the available written documentation on the validity and reliability of tests for the specific use intended. *(Primary)*

Comment:
The degree of reliability or validity required of a test depends on its role in the assessment process and the impact of the process on the parties involved. There may be situations in which, in a user's professional judgment, decisions or inferences should be based, in part, on tests for which there is little evidence of reliability or validity for the intended use. In these situations, the user should take great care not to imply that the decisions or inferences made are based on test results of known reliability or validity. When feasible, repeated use of such tests should include efforts to develop the appropriate evidence.

Standard 6.2

When a test user makes a substantial change in test format, mode of administration, instructions, language, or content, the user should revalidate the use of the test for the changed conditions or have a rationale supporting the claim that additional validation is not necessary or possible. *(Primary)*

Standard 6.3   When a test is to be used for a purpose for which it has not been previously validated, or for which there is no supported claim for validity, the user is responsible for providing evidence of validity. *(Primary)*

Comment:
The individual who makes the claim for validity is responsible for providing the necessary evidence. Evidence of validity sufficient for test use may often be obtained from a well-documented manual. If previous evidence is not sufficient, then additional data should be collected. The provisions of this standard should not be construed to prohibit the generation of hypotheses from test data. For example, though many clinical tests have limited or contradictory validity evidence for common uses, clinicians generate hypotheses based appropriately on responses to such tests. These hypotheses should, however, be labeled clearly as such.

Standard 6.4   Test users should accurately portray the relevance of a test to the assessment and decision-making process and should not use a test score to justify an evaluation, recommendation, or decision that has been made largely on some other basis. *(Primary)*

Standard 6.5   Test users should be alert to probable unintended consequences of test use and should attempt to avoid actions that have unintended negative consequences. *(Primary)*

Comment:
For example, test users should act to counter the tendency of people to attach unsupported surplus meanings to test scores. Obviously, test users cannot anticipate every unintended consequence. What is required is an attempt that is reasonable and made in good faith to avoid unintended consequences that might be anticipated.

Standard 6.6   Responsibility for test use should be assumed by or delegated only to those individuals who have the training and experience necessary to handle this responsibility in a professional and technically adequate manner. Any special qualifications for test administration or interpretation noted in the manual should be met. *(Primary)*

Comment:
This standard has special significance in areas such as clinical testing, testing for special education, testing of handicapped people, and other such situations where potential impact is great.

Standard 6.7   Test users should verify periodically that changes in populations of test takers, objectives of the testing process, or changes in available techniques have not made their current procedures inappropriate. *(Conditional)*

Standard 6.8   When test results are released to the news media, those responsible for releasing the results should provide information to help minimize the possibility of the misinterpretation of the test results. *(Primary)*

Standard 6.9   When a specific cut score is used to select, classify, or certify test takers, the method and rationale for setting that cut score, including any technical analyses, should be presented in a manual or report. When cut scores are based primarily on professional judgment, the qualifications of the judges also should be documented. *(Primary)*

Comment:
In employment and some other testing applications there may be no pre-specified cut score; the number of individuals to be selected is determined by the number of available openings.

Standard 6.10   In educational, clinical, and counseling applications, test administrators and users should not attempt to evaluate test takers whose special characteristics--ages, handicapping conditions, or linguistic, generational, or cultural backgrounds--are outside the range of their academic training or supervised experience. A test user faced with a request to evaluate a test taker whose special characteristics are not within his or her range of professional experience should seek consultation regarding test selection, necessary modifications of testing procedures, and score interpretation from a professional who has had relevant experience. *(Primary)*

Standard 6.11   In school, clinical, and counseling applications, a test taker's score should not be accepted as a reflection of lack of ability with respect to the characteristic being tested for without consideration of alternate explanations for the test taker's inability to perform on that test at that time. *(Conditional)*

Comment:
Many test manuals point out variables that should be considered in interpreting test scores, such as clinically relevant history, school record, vocational status, and examiner or test taker differences. Influences associated with variables such as socioeconomic status, ethnicity, cultural background, language, age, or gender may also be relevant. In addition, medication, visual impairments, or other handicapping conditions may affect a test taker's performance on, for example, a paper-and-pencil test of mathematics. Such alternate explanations for a test taker's level of performance should be considered before interpreting the test taker's score as reflecting ability level with respect to the skills being tested.

Standard 6.12   In school, clinical, and counseling applications, tests developed for screening should be used only for identifying test takers who may need further evaluation. The results of such tests should not be used to characterize a person or to make any decision about a person, other than the decision for referral for further evaluation, unless adequate reliability and validity for these other uses can be demonstrated. *(Primary)*

Standard 6.13   Test users should not use interpretations of test results, including computer-interpreted test results, unless they have a manual for that test that includes information on the validities of the interpretations for the intended applications and on the samples on which they were based. *(Primary)*

Comment:
The user of a special service has the obligation to be thoroughly familiar with the principles on which interpretations are derived and should have the ability to evaluate a computer-based interpretation of test performance in light of other evidence. Considerable professional judgment is needed to use computer-based interpretations appropriately.

7. Clinical Testing

Background

The use of tests as part of a clinical assessment is characterized mainly by the fact that the choice of tests is individualized and usually only one person at a time is tested. The test taker may be a child, adolescent, or adult; the setting may be a school, mental health or outpatient clinic, hospital, prison, or private practitioner's office. In any event, tests are chosen to provide information useful for assessment and decision making for that specific individual, taking into account his or her special background and characteristics.

A wide range of tests and procedures is employed, including tests of aptitudes or abilities, attitudes, and personality characteristics; projective techniques; interview schedules; checklists; behavioral observations; rating scales; and others. Tests are used to make decisions about diagnostic classification; presence of neurological impairment; suitability for particular types of treatment or educational instruction; identification of intellectual and personality assets that can be used in rehabilitative, therapeutic, or educational planning; eligibility for parole or probation; and evaluation of treatment outcomes. In many clinical situations decision making is fluid in that treatment yields additional information that can serve to modify the decisions. In other circumstances clinical testing may be involved in decisions having a powerful and lasting impact on people's lives (e.g., parole, sentencing, civil commitment, competency to stand trial, and child custody).

Projective techniques and many interview and behavioral observation techniques are often used as aids in clinical assessment and treatment selection. Each of these methods yields multiple hypotheses regarding the behavior of the subject in various situations as they arise, with each hypothesis modifiable on the basis of further information. When one of these measures is so used, interpretations are judged by its total contribution to the clinical understanding of an individual rather than by the validity of each hypothesis.

Computers are being used increasingly to administer, score, and interpret tests. However, whether clinicians do the testing themselves or employ a computer or an assistant, they have the responsibility of selecting the appropriate tests for a specific individual in accordance with that person's unique characteristics, the setting, and the nature of the question posed. Clinicians are also responsible for ensuring that the testing conditions are appropriate. For example, such matters as whether a client who needs glasses or a hearing aid has them available during testing can affect the validity of test results. Is the client capable of reading at the level required by the test? Is the test material suitable for this elderly or young client? In addition, it is the clinician's responsibility to assure confidentiality, assess the suitability of test results and computer interpretations, and communicate them in appropriate terms to the client and concerned others.

A number of special problems arise in the use of instruments for clinical assessment. Such instruments are often multiply scored. Intercorrelations among the resulting scales are often high due to the common format, item overlap, and overlapping constructs. Furthermore, even though scores may be standardized with respect to a reference group, interpretations are often based on the absolute level of standard scores or of their differences rather than on scores relative to those obtained by others. Appropriately, manuals sometimes contain the warning that score levels should be interpreted with caution and that interpretations obtained by examining several independently obtained sources is desirable.

Another area requiring special attention is that of open-ended responses. Examples of clinical instruments involving these are sentence completion forms, analyses of verbal material obtained from tape recordings or videotapes of interviews or therapy sessions, and ratings of behavior in natural or contrived settings. Special care is needed with such approaches to ensure that the instruments are administered in a facilitating atmosphere without suggestions or cues that might influence the response given, unless such prompting is specifically planned as part of the test. Furthermore, the scoring categories used in open-ended response instruments need to be defined clearly, and special training may be needed for coding the responses.

Chapter 1 describes the three categories of evidence of test validity that should be considered in interpreting test scores. Of these, construct-related evidence is of primary importance for clinical and personality tests. Interpretations of personality traits, attitudes, underlying personality tendencies, and psychiatric classifications are all constructs requiring evidence of validity. Content-related and criterion-related evidence may sometimes be a part of construct evidence.

Clinicians deal not only with the diagnostic uses of tests, but also with the prediction of behavior and with response to treatment. When clinical instruments are used in decision making, that use is constrained by the same consideration of criterion-related evidence of validity as is any other use of tests.

Standard 7.1

Clinicians should not imply that interpretations of test data are based on empirical evidence of validity unless such evidence exists for the interpretations given. *(Primary)*

Comment:
This standard should not be construed to prohibit interpretations of test data presented as hypotheses or clinical judgments.

Standard 7.2

When validity is appraised by comparing the level of agreement between test results and clinical diagnoses, the diagnostic terms or categories employed should be carefully defined or identified, and the method by which a diagnosis was made should be specified. If diagnosis was made based on judgments, information on the training, experience, and professional status of the judges and on the nature and extent of the judges' contacts with the test takers should be included. *(Primary)*

Standard 7.3

When differential diagnosis is needed, the user should choose, if possible, a test for which there is evidence of the test's ability to distinguish between the two or more diagnostic groups of concern rather than merely to distinguish abnormal cases from the general population. *(Primary)*

Comment:
Test users will find it particularly helpful if validity information is in a form that enables them to determine how much confidence can be placed in judgments regarding an individual. Differences between group means and their statistical significance give inadequate information regarding validity for diagnostic purposes. Further information might consist of a table showing the degree of overlap of predictor distributions among different criterion groups.

Standard 7.4	Test users should determine from the manual or other reported evidence whether the construct being measured corresponds to the nature of the assessment that is intended. *(Primary)*

Standard 7.5	Clinicians should share with their clients test results and interpretations, as well as information about the range of error for such interpretations when such information will be beneficial to the client. Such information should be expressed in language that the client (or client's legal representative) can understand. *(Secondary)*

Standard 7.6	Criterion-related evidence of validity for populations similar to that for which the test will be used should be available when recommendations or decisions are presented as having an actuarial, as well as a clinical, basis. *(Primary)*

8. Educational Testing and Psychological Testing in the Schools

Background

Testing in education is pervasive. From pre-kindergarten readiness assessments to professional specialty licensing and certification, students participate in a continuing testing and evaluation process designed to monitor their progress, to provide a basis for selection into programs with limited enrollment, and for the award of certificates of qualification. This chapter covers four areas of application: school testing programs, educational certification testing, educational selection, and special education. Chapters 7, 13, and 14 also contain material relevant to educational testing. The use of tests in counseling is covered in Chapter 9 and test use in program evaluation is covered in Chapter 12.

School Testing Programs

Since the early part of this century, school testing programs have been integral to elementary and secondary education. Each year millions of students in thousands of public and private schools take group standardized tests of ability and achievement chosen and administered by their schools, districts, or states. These school testing programs provide local test users with information about the ability and achievement levels of individual students and of groups of students aggregated at various levels.

The test results are used by school administrators, teachers, parents, students, various citizen groups, and the media. The results of carefully selected, appropriate tests, when interpreted properly, can provide administrators with pertinent information about the general academic development and level of functioning of individual students, thereby helping to provide students with appropriate instruction and resources. Test scores can help teachers, students, and parents identify the specific academic strengths of a student on which to build, as well as the specific less-developed areas in need of remediation and special attention.

Other people use test scores as part of formal or informal evaluations of the effectiveness of the school, district, or state in educating students. Often test results on a school-by-school basis are reported by the local news media without comment or explanation of the possible reasons for any differences that may exist between schools within the district. This practice tends to contribute significantly to the misinterpretation and misuse of test results.

The group of users associated with school testing programs is perhaps the largest and most heterogeneous of all user groups. These diverse users should be provided help in interpreting test results. The job may be made easier by using material developed by publishers, but care must be taken to assure that such materials can be understood and are appropriate for local conditions.

Certification Testing in Elementary and Secondary Education

The use of educational certification tests in both elementary and secondary schools has grown rapidly over the past few years at both the state and local levels. "Educational certification test" is a generic term that applies to many different uses of test results and perhaps obscures the considerable diversity among programs. Students' scores on educational certification tests are used either alone or in conjunction with other criteria to make decisions concerning high school graduation or grade-to-grade promotion, to classify students for remediation, to evaluate the effectiveness of schools, to classify or certify school districts, to allocate compensatory funds or other resources to districts, and to evaluate teachers.

An important use of educational certification tests is in the awarding of high school diplomas. In some jurisdictions, if students cannot pass the test, they may receive a certificate of attendance instead of the regular diploma. In others, students who pass the educational certification test receive an endorsed diploma, and those who fail the test, but have met all of the other graduation requirements, are awarded a regular diploma. In some jurisdictions students may earn the high school diploma by passing a test before completing all courses normally required for graduation, and for many years adults have used tests as an alternate route to the high school credential.

Using test scores for classification or certification decisions (i.e., Does the student need remediation? Should the student be promoted or graduated?) presupposes a consensual body of material upon which all students can be reasonably compared. This body of material to which all students have been exposed consists usually of a set of standard textbooks or curricular material, but systematic instruction and a minimum period of study for all students are also implied.

Most educational certification testing programs use a predetermined cut score to distinguish passing from failing scores. The cut score becomes the linchpin in the decision process. Research has shown that there can be large discrepancies between the cut scores produced by the most common methods of setting cut scores. Therefore, the reliability and validity of decisions and inferences based on cut scores from educational certification tests need to be studied carefully.

The agency that mandates an educational certification program, usually the state legislature or the state or local board of education, frequently functions as both the test developer and the test user. Often the agency enters into a contract with a test company to construct a test according to agreed-upon specifications. In such situations the agency is still technically the test developer, even though an external organization actually builds the test. The agency mandating the test and the test development contractor should collaborate to ensure provision of the documentation that permits an evaluation of the degree to which appropriate standards of test development, validity, and reliability have been followed.

Educational Selection

Admissions requirements vary widely among undergraduate colleges and universities, as well as among graduate and professional schools. Competitive admissions, often involving testing, is also becoming increasingly common in elementary and secondary schools. At the undergraduate level, the degree of selectivity ranges from open-door policies that admit any high school graduate (or applicant with equivalent credentials) to highly selective institutions that require considerable evidence of outstanding academic ability and superior past performance. Not only do the requirements vary from institution to institution but also from one specialization to another within an institution. At the graduate level, requirements may differ for applicants to the same department depending on their proposed areas of specialization.

Despite the diversity in how selection testing is used, there are substantial similarities among selection processes. Several types of information are typically required. These may include past academic record (e.g., transcripts, grade-point average, or rank in class), test scores, letters of recommendation, lists of past accomplishments, and statements by the applicant (e.g., goals, personal description, or a writing sample). Descriptive background data such as gender, age, and racial or ethnic group designation are also frequently requested and may be used for affirmative action or other purposes. This list is not intended to be exhaustive or to apply to all institutions, but it does show some of the range.

Criterion-related evidence is the most common approach to validation in admissions contexts, although content-related and construct-related evidence are important. It should be noted that many institutions select students in order to meet other types of objectives besides that of achieving academic excellence, a fact that needs to be taken into account in assessing the validity of the test application.

The results of criterion-related validation studies need to be interpreted in the context of previous results at the individual institution and results obtained at other similar institutions. Results for other similar institutions are most relevant in schools or colleges where the number of students available for a criterion-related validity study is small. Results for a single small sample at a particular school or college may be much less informative than results accumulated across many similar institutions.

A logical analysis of the types of questions and the processes necessary to answer those questions is a necessary part of evaluating the validity of a test. The question of whether coaching alters the meaning of the scores provides a useful example. An interpretation that says that a test measures abilities that are developed over the course of many years and that those abilities change slowly as the result of time and effort would be called into question by evidence of significant changes that result from short-term coaching. In general, if the changes are large, the coaching period is relatively short, and the coaching itself deals with essentially nonacademic tasks such as test-taking skills or anxiety, then the validity of the test interpretation is called into question. On the other hand, evidence that coaching results in changes not only in test performance but also in other indicators of academic performance, such as subsequent grades, would help support the validity of the interpretation, especially if the coaching was relatively long term and dealt with the acquisition of academic skills and knowledge.

Special Education

Tests are used in special education to aid in clarifying the types, bases, and extent of an individual test taker's learning difficulties or school adjustment problems. Ultimately, the test results are used in planning an individual education program for the student, sometimes including placement in a special school or classroom. A variety of types of tests is used in special education, including, but not limited to, learning aptitude tests, group or individual achievement tests, tests of specific skills thought to be basic to school learning (e.g., visual-motor integration skills), speech and language tests, vision and hearing tests, personality inventories, behavioral observations, and projective techniques.

In special education, tests are selected, administered, and interpreted by school psychologists, classroom teachers, special educators, and other professionals, such as speech pathologists and physical therapists. This diverse group of test users includes professionals with varying levels of training in measurement and evaluation and with varying degrees of technical expertise in testing. When test users in special education have little or no training in measurement principles, the risk of test misuse is high.

Legislation now requires school officials to evaluate large numbers of children, including children with whom they have not typically had assessment experience--children with low-incidence severe handicaps, preschool children, and people 18 to 21 years of age. This mandated increase in testing, the pressure of time (evaluations must be completed within a specific number of working days after referral), and economic implications (the school is responsible for whatever special education services the evaluation results suggest are needed) have created pressures toward expediency in testing practices. For example, there may be administrative pressure to use less expensive, less time-consuming, or more readily available testing procedures than the test administrator believes are warranted. There may also be pressures not to look for, or not to find, problems that require expensive services, and this may affect, to some extent, the interpretation of test results. In addition, pressures may lead to the use of available but inadequately trained staff to evaluate populations of children with whom they have not previously had experience. Although school staff may be knowledgeable about the assessment of mildly and moderately disabled children of ages 5 to 18, they may not be trained or experienced in the evaluation of the younger, older, or more severely handicapped children who must now be evaluated according to law.

Adhering to professional testing standards in special education is increasingly important in the face of these pressures toward expediency. Strict adherence is necessary in those situations in which test-based decisions will have substantial impact on a child's education and life--situations in which special class or school placement is at issue.

Service Delivery to Regular Education

School psychologists employ a wide range of individually administered tests in the process of service delivery to students in regular education classes. These services are for students who may not have special education needs, but have behavioral, emotional, and/or learning problems sufficiently intense to frustrate their educational development, and often the educational development of others. Test results are one source of data in the evaluation of such students.

Standard 8.1

Those responsible for school testing programs should ensure that the individuals who administer the tests are properly instructed in the appropriate test administration procedures and that they understand the importance of adhering to the directions for administration that are provided by the test developer. *(Primary)*

Standard 8.2

Those responsible for school testing programs should ensure that the individuals who use the test scores within the school context are properly instructed in the appropriate methods for interpreting test scores. *(Primary)*

Comment:
The interpretation of some test results is sufficiently complex to require that the user have relevant psychological training and experience. Examples of such tests include personality inventories, projective techniques, and neuropsychological tests. Administering and interpreting individually administered intelligence tests also requires extensive training and experience.

Standard 8.3

If test results are used in making statements about the differences between aptitude and achievement for an individual student, any educational decision based on these differences should take into account the overlap between the constructs and the reliability or standard error of the difference score. *(Primary)*

Comment:
It should not be assumed that, because the words "aptitude" or "ability" are used in the title of a test, it measures a construct distinct from what is measured by an "achievement" test.

Standard 8.4

When a test is to be used to certify the successful completion of a given level of education, either grade-to-grade promotion or high school graduation, both the test domain and the instructional domain at the given level of education should be described in sufficient detail, without compromising test security, so that the agreement between the test domain and the content domain can be evaluated. *(Primary)*

Standard 8.5	When a test is developed by a state or local district to be used for student promotion, graduation, or classification decisions, user's guides, or technical reports should be developed and disseminated. *(Conditional)*

Comment:
An agency that develops a certification or classification test has the same obligation to supply a manual and technical reports as does a commercial test publisher. A test that is widely used throughout a jurisdiction, even though not published or sold, requires a technical manual so that it can be properly used and evaluated. In smaller testing programs, dissemination may be limited to summary statements, provided that detailed analyses are made available on request.

Standard 8.6	Results from certification tests should be reported promptly to all appropriate parties, including students, parents, and teachers. The report should contain a description of the test, what is measured, the conclusions and decisions that are based on the test results, the obtained score, information on how to interpret the reported score, and any cut score used for classification. *(Primary)*

Standard 8.7	When a test is used to make decisions about student promotion or graduation, there should be evidence that the test covers only the specific or generalized knowledge, skills, and abilities that students have had the opportunity to learn. *(Primary)*

Standard 8.8	Students who must demonstrate mastery of certain skills or knowledge before being promoted or granted a diploma should have multiple opportunities to demonstrate the skills. *(Primary)*

Standard 8.9	Relationships between predictors and criterion measures that are used in educational admissions should be described by regression equations and associated standard errors of estimate or by expectancy tables in addition to correlation coefficients. *(Primary)*

Standard 8.10	The possibility that differential prediction exists in educational selection for selected groups should be investigated where there is prior evidence to suggest that positive results may be found and where sample sizes are adequate. *(Conditional)*

Comment:
The difficulty posed by small samples is particularly acute for questions of differential prediction among some groups. Native Americans, for example, form such a small fraction of the overall population that few schools can be expected to have enough students for an adequate differential prediction study. Thus, the only feasible way of addressing the question is through cooperative efforts by many institutions that allow combining information across institutions.

Standard 8.11

Test users should not imply that empirical evidence exists for a relationship among particular test results, prescribed educational plans, and desired student outcomes unless such evidence is available. *(Primary)*

Comment:
Test results in special education are often used to develop specific educational objectives and instructional strategies that are assumed to remediate a student's educational deficits or to enable the student to compensate for them. This assumes a relationship among test results and instructional technologies that may not have been demonstrated. In some cases there is limited empirical evidence for a relationship among test results, instructional strategies, and student achievement outcomes.

When evidence supporting the utility of testing procedures for instructional purposes is lacking, test users can stress the tentative nature of the recommendations they provide and encourage teachers and others to weigh the usefulness of that information in light of additional available data.

Standard 8.12

In elementary or secondary education, a decision or characterization that will have a major impact on a test taker should not automatically be made on the basis of a single test score. Other relevant information for the decision should also be taken into account by the professionals making the decision. *(Primary)*

Comment:
A student should not be placed in special classes or schools, for example, solely on the basis of an ability test score. Other information about the student's ability to learn, such as observations by teachers or parents, should also play a part in such decisions.

9. Test Use in Counseling

Uses of tests in counseling differ from most other test uses in that the test taker is viewed as the primary user of test results. Accumulated experience and research evidence have shown that standardized tests can be a valuable part of the counseling process. If used appropriately, tests can provide useful information to clients. However, because test takers do not typically have professional testing knowledge and skill, they need assistance and guidance from counselors and developers of interpretive materials who have a unique role in facilitating the appropriate and effective use of tests.

Counselors are concerned with a range of assessment and guidance activities related to the life-span development and decision-making activities of individuals. Typical counseling concerns include the individual's personal and social skills, educational achievement, developed abilities, educational and vocational interests, occupational knowledge and preferences, occupational values, career development, study skills, coping and problem solving skills, and plans and values for other important roles in adult life, such as relationships with others, work, and parenting. These characteristics of the individual are assessed in counseling by a variety of formal and informal procedures--paper-and-pencil inventories, tests, work samples, interviews, card sorts, checklists, and so on. All such measures that yield classifications and raw or converted scores that result in suggestions for exploration or recommendations for action are considered tests and require evidence of reliability and validity.

Counselors work in a variety of settings: schools, government, industry, agencies, and private practice. They may assist individuals in examining educational, career, work, family, leisure, and retirement choices. One important function in schools is that of consulting with administrators, teachers, parents, and students to assist individual students in the selection of educational programs. When tests are an important part of the decision process, the tests may, in effect, become the basis for the placement of students. School counselors may play a similar role in assisting individuals in choosing colleges and in making decisions about college programs. In these cases the standards for the use of tests in educational classification and placement may be appropriate.

All interpretive reports, whether provided in printed form or on video display terminals, are an extension of the individual profiles and score reports that are part of the counseling testing program. They may be used to provide the results of tests to students and parents, as well as to professional staff. Depending on the availability of counselors and other school staff who are trained in test interpretation and use, students who receive computer-based interpretation reports may or may not receive further interpretation of such reports. For many tests used in schools, therefore, test developers need to take into account the likelihood that students will receive little or no professional assistance in interpreting test results other than that provided by the computer-based interpretation reports. The test taker, who has no technical training in testing, must be able to interpret and use test information accurately and must depend largely on materials accompanying the computer-based interpretation report. The developers of such tests or computer-based interpretations should provide comprehensive and easily understandable interpretive and instructional material.

Computer-assisted guidance systems are also within the scope of the *Standards*. These systems may incorporate test-like tasks or existing interest or ability measures. Results of rating scales, ability measures, or estimates may be used to structure the search for occupations. Occupations are sometimes presented or recommended to users on the basis of measures of occupational attributes. Manuals should spell out the procedures by which occupational characteristics were developed, the system by which occupational attributes were linked to individual characteristics, and evidence on the validity of particular recommendations.

Test interpretations and test uses in counseling for vocational, career, and life development are influenced by the experiences of the individual test taker and of the professionals who provide information in this process. To some degree these experiences, in interactions with peers and adults and in schools and other settings, have been group-linked and related to fixed characteristics of individuals (e.g., gender, race or ethnicity, or socio-economic background). Test interpretation and test use may similarly be limited by perceptions and experiences related to group membership. This issue is of particular concern in uses of tests in counseling. Both counselor and test taker should consider whether learning experiences leading to the development of preferences and competencies have been stereotyped by expectations of behaviors considered appropriate for females and males, for racial and ethnic minorities, based on socioeconomic status, or for people with handicapping conditions.

Standard 9.1

Testing for counseling should have as its primary goals the acquisition of relevant information and the reporting of that information with appropriate interpretations so that clients from diverse backgrounds can be assisted in making important educational, personal, and career decisions. *(Primary)*

Standard 9.2

Counselors should review the interpretive materials provided to clients to evaluate accuracy, clarity, and usefulness of the materials. Manuals for tests or computer-based interpretations should be evaluated for evidence for the validity of specific interpretations made. *(Primary)*

Comment:
A counselor should determine, for example, whether classifications for particular vocational courses are based on cut scores supported by evidence of successful course completion or on other criteria. Are occupational suggestions based on empirical study of people entering the occupations? The bases of such interpretations should be stated clearly, perhaps by presenting expectancy tables or probability statements. For some tests this information may vary for groups of test takers. Qualified professional users should have access to explicit information on the accuracy of the classifications used as the basis of interpretations. If data to support such interpretive statements have not been collected, that fact should be stated clearly.

Standard 9.3

Counselors should review technical data and develop a rationale for the decision to use combined or separate norms for females and males in reports to test takers. *(Primary)*

Comment:
This standard is concerned with the possible effect of prior experience on present choices. For example, in tests that are used for choosing vocational courses, scores for female test takers may reflect present status but may not predict future performance in a vocational course. One way to examine this possibility is to compare an individual's standing relative to others in the same gender group. Comparing both norm groups provides an opportunity to discuss the influence of prior

experiences on test scores and to assess the accuracy of the score for an individual student.

For some interest inventories, not all occupational scales will have both female and male criterion-group norms. However, providing scores on all scales, based on clearly identified female or male criterion groups, facilitates the counseling use of the inventory with all clients.

Standard 9.4

If a publisher packages tests that are to be used in combination for counseling, the counselor should review the manual for the rationale for the specific combination of tests used and the justification of the interpretive relationships among the scores. *(Primary)*

Comment:
For example, if measures of developed abilities (e.g., achievement or specific or general abilities) are used with interest measures to suggest a requisite combination of scores for success, then supporting validity data for this combination should be available.

Standard 9.5

Counselors should examine test manuals for any available information about how suggested or implied career options (i.e., the vocational program or occupation suggested by the highest scores on the test) are distributed for samples of the typical respondents of each gender and relevant racial or ethnic groups. *(Primary)*

Standard 9.6

Counselors should review the test materials that are provided to the test takers to be sure that such materials properly caution the test taker not to rely on the test scores solely when making life-planning decisions. The counselor should encourage the test taker to consider other relevant information on personal and social skills, values, interests, accomplishments, experiences, and on other test scores and observations. *(Primary)*

Comment:
It is important to recognize that vocational interests, abilities, and choices may be influenced by environmental and cultural factors, including early socialization, traditional sex-role expectations of society, and the experiences typical of members of various gender, racial, ethnic, handicapped, and socioeconomic groups. For example, female clients in general may have had fewer science- and mathematics-related experiences. Counselors in some instances may suggest and encourage exploratory experiences in those areas where interests have not had a chance to develop. For many high school students particularly, test results should be used to expand options rather than to narrow options prematurely.

Standard 9.7

Counselors should encourage multiple valid assessments of an individual's abilities, social skills, and interests. *(Primary)*

Comment:
School or work performance, extracurricular activities, and hobbies are examples of indicators that might be used to lessen a test user's and a test taker's reliance on a single measure of important characteristics.

Standard 9.8 Counselors should review the interpretive materials for ability or interest measures and for other tests that are used with people who are reentering employment or education or changing work settings for their appropriateness for these clients. A counselor should consider the age, experience, and background of the client as they are compared with the characteristics of the norm groups on which the scores are based. *(Primary)*

Comment:
For example, for the majority of inventories and ability tests, normative data are based on younger test takers. Although these tests may be useful with older test takers, scores should be interpreted cautiously.

Standard 9.9 Counselors should review interpretive materials for tests to ensure that case studies and examples are not limited to illustrations of people in traditional roles. *(Secondary)*

Comment:
For example, counselors might look for case studies and examples of men and women of different ages, and in different ethnic, racial, or handicapped groups. Where tests are used widely in adult counseling, such as for men and women reentering education or the labor force or changing careers, case studies and examples that are relevant for these clients should be sought.

10. Employment Testing

Background

The standards presented in this chapter are those that are more specific to the use of tests and inventories in employment selection, promotion, and classification in civilian and military organizations. These standards are designed to be consistent with the general standards for test construction, reliability, validity, and test use that have been discussed in earlier chapters.

In employment settings tests may be used in conjunction with other information to make predictions or decisions about individual personnel actions. The principal obligation of employment testing is to produce reasonable evidence for the validity of such predictions and decisions.

Issues relevant to decision-theoretic models are directly applicable. For example, the relative frequency of various kinds of decision errors, the utility of a correct decision (and the value judgments which that utility determination entails), comparisons of alternate strategies, and the availability of prior information are all relevant considerations. Competent use of tests in employment settings depends on sound professional judgment to take these considerations into account formally or informally, as is appropriate. The major kinds of decisions to which tests might contribute in this setting are the following:

1. Selecting individuals for an entry level position.
2. Making differential job assignments based on test data (classification).
3. Selecting individuals for advanced or specialized positions.
4. Promoting individuals from within an organization to higher level positions (as when test information collected at an assessment center is used to make promotion decisions).
5. Deciding who is eligible for training on the basis of a test of prerequisites.
6. Using tests or inventories as diagnostic tools to aid in planning job and career development for individuals.

Competent test use can make significant and demonstrable contributions to productivity and to fair treatment of individuals in employment settings. Among available alternatives, tests are the most valid and the least discriminatory personnel decision aids available.

Large organizations are likely to have more resources than are smaller organizations to devote to test development or test validation. More funds and professional staff may be available, and more job holders may be available to use as research participants. Where resources or sample sizes are limited, the criterion-related evidence of validity and content-related validation judgments obtained on similar jobs in other settings and the strength of the construct-related evidence of validity already generated by the test become particularly important. Employers should not be precluded from using a test if it can be demonstrated that the test has generated a significant record of validity in similar job settings for highly similar people or that it is otherwise appropriate to generalize from other applications.

Promotion decisions are distinguished from selection decisions largely by the fact that the individual who is being considered for promotion has an established job performance record in the organization. Thus, the employer may know considerably more about that individual than is known about new applicants. An employer will need to decide to what extent job performance information should be combined with test information.

Tests are frequently used systematically to make classification or placement decisions in military employment, but rarely are they used as such in civilian employment. For example, the aim might be to hire and assign individuals to different jobs in order to maximize the overall criterion performance of the whole group, or individuals might be assigned to different levels of a training program based on how they score on a test of their qualifications. In general, the justification for using tests to make such decisions rests on demonstrating some degree of differential validity among job assignments.

Standard 10.1

Criterion-related validity in a current situation should be inferred from a single previous validation study only if the previous criterion-related study was done under favorable conditions (i.e., with a large sample size and a good criterion) and if the current situation has a close correspondence with the previous situation. *(Conditional)*

Comment:
Close correspondence means that the job duties and requirements or underlying psychological constructs are substantially the same (as is determined by a job analysis), that the predictor is the same (i.e., the test is the same), and that the level of performance required is substantially the same.

Standard 10.2

If tests are to be used to make job classification decisions (e.g., the pattern of predictor scores will be used to make differential job assignments), evidence of differential prediction among jobs or job groups should be documented. *(Secondary)*

Standard 10.3

The rationale for criterion relevance should be made explicit. It should include a description of the job in question and of the judgments used to determine relevance. *(Primary)*

Comment:
In general, the judged relevance of a criterion should flow directly from the link between the behaviors or other elements assessed by the criterion and the goals of the organization. It should reflect important and substantial aspects of the job. Also, the purposes to be served by the criteria and the purposes of the validation study should be stated clearly. The goal of job performance criterion measurement is to represent the major factors that reflect an individual's contribution to the organization. However, breadth of coverage cannot always be the sole consideration: Comprehensiveness should be balanced against sound measurement. It is unwise to strive for comprehensiveness if it may seriously compromise the reliability of the major criterion factors that can be assessed or if it would introduce significant bias.

Standard 10.4

Content validation should be based on a thorough and explicit definition of the content domain of interest. For job selection, classification, and promotion, the characterization of the domain should be based on job analysis. *(Conditional)*

Comment:
In general, the job content domain should be described by characteristics that (a) can be represented in test content, (b) will not change

substantially over a specified period of time, and (c) the applicant should possess when being considered for employment.

Standard 10.5	**When the content-related validation evidence is to stand as support for the use of a test in selection or promotion, a close link between test content and job content should be demonstrated.** *(Primary)*

Comment:
For example, if the test content samples job tasks with considerable fidelity (e.g., actual job samples such as machine operation) or, in the judgment of experts, correctly simulates job task content (e.g., certain assessment center exercises), or samples specific job knowledge required for successful job performance (e.g., information necessary to exhibit certain skills), then content-related validity can be offered as the principal form of evidence of validity. If the link between the test content and the job content is not singular and direct, additional evidence is required.

Standard 10.6	**When content-related evidence of validity is presented, the rationale for defining and describing a specific job content domain in a particular way (e.g., in terms of tasks to be performed or knowledge, skills, abilities, or other personal characteristics) should be stated clearly. The rationale should establish that the knowledge, skills, and abilities said to define the domain are the major determinants of proficiency in that domain.** *(Primary)*

Comment:
When content-related evidence of validity is presented for a job or class of jobs, the evidence should include a description of the major job characteristics that a test is meant to sample, including the relative frequency or criticality of the elements. The supporting argument might be provided by additional construct-related evidence of validity or by appropriate kinds of job analysis data.

Standard 10.7	**If the validity of a test for selection into a particular job is based on content-related evidence, a similar inference should be made about the test in a new situation only if the critical job content factors are substantially the same (as is determined by a job analysis), the reading level of the test material does not exceed that appropriate for the new applicant group and the new job, and there are no discernible features of the new situation that would substantially change the original meaning of the test material.** *(Conditional)*

Standard 10.8	**If construct-related evidence is to be the major support of validity for personnel selection, two links need to be established. First, there should be evidence for the validity of the test as a measure of the construct, and second, there should be evidence for the validity of the construct as a determinant of major factors of job performance. There should be a clear conceptual rationale for this linkage. Both the construct and the job factors to which it is to be linked should be defined carefully. A consistent pattern of results should point toward the hypothesized relationship. Expert judgment alone should not be used to substantiate a claim of construct-related evidence.** *(Primary)*

Standard 10.9   A clear explanation should be given of any technical basis for any cut score used to make personnel decisions. Cut scores should not be set solely on the basis of recommendations made in the test manual. *(Primary)*

11. Professional and Occupational Licensure and Certification

Background

Tests have played an important role in licensure and certification for some occupations for many years. As regulation by state governments has expanded to cover increasing numbers of occupations, so too has the use of tests. Several hundred occupations are now regulated by state governments. Many other occupations are certified by nongovernmental agencies. The range of occupations covered by some form of licensure or certification is wide, including traditional professions such as medicine, psychology, law, and teaching, as well as technical and specialized occupations, such as air traffic control, computer programming, cosmetology, physical therapy, laboratory technology, auto mechanics, and real estate.

The primary purpose of licensure or certification is to protect the public. Licensing requirements are imposed to ensure that those licensed possess knowledge and skills in sufficient degree to perform important occupational activities safely and effectively. The purpose of certification is to provide the public (including employers and government agencies) with a dependable mechanism for identifying practitioners who have met particular standards. At one time it was widely accepted that the distinction between licensing and certification was that the former usually set minimum (entry-level) standards, whereas the latter set standards well above the minimum. This is still the classical distinction. In recent years, however, this distinction has been blurred because many certification agencies have set their standards at the entry level. Defining the level of competence required for licensing or certification is one of the most important and difficult tasks facing those responsible for such programs.

Many occupational groups rely on national testing organizations to develop the examinations that are used for certification or licensure. Other groups have developed their own tests by employing professional staff with expertise in measurement. These examinations are frequently developed by boards consisting largely of members of the profession. The types of examinations vary widely, including traditional tests using multiple-choice questions, written essay exams, oral exams, and performance tests (e.g., flying an airplane or filling a tooth while being observed by one or more examiners).

Issues of validity that are discussed in other sections of the *Standards* are also relevant to testing for licensure and certification. Although many of the issues of central importance in the present context are discussed in the chapter on employment testing, some important distinctions must be made. For licensure or certification the focus of test standards is on levels of knowledge and skills necessary to assure the public that a person is competent to practice, whereas an employer may use tests in order to maximize productivity. Investigations of criterion-related validity are more problematic in the context of licensure or certification than in many employment settings. Not all those certified or licensed are necessarily hired; those hired are likely to be in a variety of job assignments with many different employers, and some may be self-employed. These factors often make traditional studies that gather criterion-related evidence of validity infeasible.

The difficulty in conducting criterion-related validation studies does not, however, lessen the importance of validity, which remains a central concern. Test users should develop the evidential basis to support a particular use. For licensure and certification, however, primary reliance must usually be placed on content evidence that is supplemented by evidence of the appropriateness of the construct being measured.

The process of determining a cut score for licensure and certification examinations is different from that in employee and student selection. Tests are used in licensure or certification to help ensure that those certified or licensed meet or exceed a standard or specified level of performance in order to be licensed or certified. There is not an explicit limit on the number of people that can be considered qualified. Cut scores associated with selection or classification uses of tests, on the other hand, are influenced by supply and demand; that is, the number of available openings affects the score level used in selection or hiring. Test takers may simply be rank-ordered by their scores and the cut score determined by the number of available openings.

Whereas employment tests may measure appropriately an individual's aptitude to learn a specific job, people who take licensure or certification tests have usually completed training and are seeking to be deemed qualified for a broad field, rather than for a specific job. This distinction has important implications for the content to be covered in licensing or certification tests.

Standard 11.1

The content domain to be covered by a licensure or certification test should be defined clearly and explained in terms of the importance of the content for competent performance in an occupation. A rationale should be provided to support a claim that the knowledge or skills being assessed are required for competent performance in an occupation and are consistent with the purpose for which the licensing or certification program was instituted. *(Primary)*

Comment:
Job analyses provide the primary basis for defining the content domain. If a single examination is used in the licensure or certification of people employed in a variety of settings and specializations, a number of jobs may need to be analyzed. Although the job analysis techniques are comparable to those used in employment testing, the emphasis for licensure and certification is limited appropriately to knowledge and skills necessary to protect the public. Generally, knowledge and skills contained in a core curriculum designed to train people for the job or occupation are relevant.

Skills that may be important to success but are not directly related to the purpose of licensure (i.e., protecting the public) should not be included in a licensing exam. For example, in real estate, marketing skills may be important for success as a broker, and assessment of these skills might have utility for agencies selecting brokers for employment. However, lack of these skills may not present a threat to the public and would appropriately be excluded from consideration for a licensing examination. The fact that successful practitioners possess certain knowledge or skills is relevant but not persuasive. Such information needs to be coupled with an analysis of the purpose of a licensing or certification program and the reasons that the knowledge or skill is required in an occupation.

Standard 11.2

Any construct interpretations of tests used for licensure and certification should be made explicit, and the evidence and logical analyses supporting these interpretations should be reported. *(Primary)*

Comment:
The claim that a particular skill is necessary for competent practice in a profession involves inferences that should be supported by evidence and logical analysis. Good performance on a certification examination should not require more reading ability, for example, than is necessary in the

occupation. The job analysis procedures used in establishing the content-related validity of a test can also contribute to the construct interpretation. One may show, for example, that qualified experts helped to define the job, identify the knowledge and skills required for competent performance, and determine the appropriate level of complexity at which these knowledges and skills should be assessed.

Standard 11.3

Estimates of the reliability of licensure or certification decisions should be provided. *(Primary)*

Comment:
The standards for decision reliability described in Chapter 2 are applicable to tests used for licensure and certification. Other types of reliability estimates and associated standard errors of measurement may also be useful, but the reliability of the decision of whether or not to certify is of primary importance.

Standard 11.4

Test takers who fail a test should, upon request, be told their score and the minimum score required to pass the test. Test takers should be given information on their performance in parts of the test for which separate scores or reports are produced and used in the decision process. *(Primary)*

Standard 11.5

Rules and procedures used to combine scores or other assessments to determine the overall outcome should be reported to test takers preferably before the test is administered. *(Secondary)*

Comment:
In some cases candidates may be required to score above a specified minimum on each of several tests. In other cases the pass-fail decision may be based solely on a total composite score.

12. Program Evaluation

The use of tests in program evaluation is commonplace at the local, state, and federal levels in education, social work, clinical psychology, corrections, and many other human service areas. Policy decision makers use test results increasingly both to inform policy and as administrative mechanisms in the implementation of policy. This chapter is limited to a consideration of the use of tests in program evaluation and policy decision making. It does not deal with such important and related issues as evaluating antecedents, inputs, or processes, which may be the focus of an evaluation.

Tests used as an integral part of program evaluation are designed to assess the effectiveness of a wide variety of programs ranging from large-scale, government-sponsored educational interventions to small-scale, developmental projects. In many instances, test use in program evaluation is mandated either by legislative action or executive agency guidelines and regulations. Tests are used widely in the implementation of statewide or district-wide needs assessment programs. In addition, tests are used as outcome measures in evaluating whether programs are being operated competently and efficiently. The types of tests used include some well-known ones, such as standardized tests of academic achievement or measures of clinical improvement, as well as some not so well known, such as measures of functional and social mobility of the elderly and chronically ill and measures of economic well-being.

Whereas an individual person is most often the focus of testing, the program is the object of interest in program evaluation. The test scores are important in the aggregate as evidence about the effectiveness of a program. It is difficult to separate matters of test use from issues of design and statistical analysis in program and project evaluation, particularly since the resulting inferences depend on all three. Study design and analysis are not considered in this chapter. The user of the *Standards* should, however, be aware that the issues are often interactive and should keep this in mind when evaluating the validity of interpretations from test data about programs or curricular materials.

Interpretations of test scores in program evaluation are problematic because the scores reflect not only the effects of particular programs or treatments, but also the individuals' lifelong history of development. Variation in test scores may be attributable to factors unrelated to the program, and the effects of such factors should be removed through research design and statistical analysis. For example, in evaluating a program to curtail violence among inmates in a correctional institution, a test of impulse control may be used to compare an experimental group and a control group. Impulse control might be expected to be related to an inmate's offense history, incarceration experience, and other personal history characteristics. Because the experiences of the experimental group and the control group may be different, a simple comparison of the outcomes for the two groups would be misleading.

Furthermore, difficulties in interpreting tests are encountered when tests or test results are used by managers and policy makers as an administrative mechanism or as a regulatory device in implementing programs or policies. For example, tests are sometimes used to allocate funds to school districts for compensatory education: Districts receive money for each student whose score falls below a certain point on the score distribution. Student test results are sometimes also used to evaluate teachers, to accredit schools or school districts, or are used for other accountability purposes. Census tracts or other political units may receive resources based on measures of need. Such uses of tests do not take into consideration the skills of the target individuals at the beginning of the school year or the histories of those individuals. Test scores cannot be used to distinguish, for example, between students who perform poorly because they have not received proper instruction and students who perform poorly because of physical, emotional, or environmental factors. Similarly, measures of the use of controlled substances cannot distinguish between use that is affected by a prevention program and use that is influenced by peers or other factors.

Standard 12.1	**Evidence of the validity and suitability of tests for the purposes of the evaluation and the populations involved should be provided.** *(Primary)*

Comment:
A justification for the use of a particular test should be given so that it is possible to judge the appropriateness of the test and the validity of inferences about a program based on test performance. Factors to be considered in selecting a test, in addition to group and individual psychometric properties, include cost, ease of administration, time constraints, and characteristics of the group (i.e., handicapping condition, native language, ethnicity, etc.). When two or more programs are being compared, the objectives of each program and the kinds of comparisons that will be made in the analysis of the data should be taken into account in selecting the tests. Tests should ordinarily be chosen for a program evaluation because of the match between the test content and the objectives of the program, project, or curriculum. However, a test may sometimes be employed precisely because it measures objectives not specifically a part of the program being evaluated so that alternate costs or positive and negative unintended outcomes can be gauged.

Standard 12.2	**When change or growth scores are used in an evaluation, the definition of change or growth and the derived score that is used to measure it should be made explicit. These definitions should be explained in terms of how the definition of growth chosen, the particular question asked, and the underlying scales used to assess growth match.** *(Primary)*

Standard 12.3	**Gain scores should not be calculated when using tests that have been modified between administrations, unless scores on the modified test have been equated to scores on the original test.** *(Primary)*

Comment:
This standard is applicable to a wide range of measures including measures of employability, job readiness, drug or controlled substance use, as well as to standardized measures of ability or achievement.

Standard 12.4	**The methods used to aggregate test results from an individual level to a group level should be described clearly.** *(Primary)*

Comment:
The aggregation method that is used will influence the description of needs and outcomes in an evaluation, the size of estimated program effects, and the inferences and legitimacy of statistical tests.

68

Standard 12.5	When describing the effectiveness of a program in terms of gains, information should be provided about gains as a function of initial scores, about changes in the number of participants scoring below specified derived scores, or about the distribution of scores, as is appropriate. *(Secondary)*

Standard 12.6	In educational program evaluation, the rationale for and method of merging the scores of students who tested out-of-grade-level, if any, with the scores of those who tested on-level should be described in the evaluation report. *(Primary)*

Standard 12.7	Evaluations of service providers (e.g., teachers and health and social service staff) and administrators should not rest exclusively on the test scores of those people that they serve. *(Primary)*

Comment:
Test scores of individuals served (e.g., students), will be affected by a great many factors not directly related to the quality of service they receive. |

Standard 12.8	When test results are used wholly or in part to allocate funds to geographic or political jurisdictions, such as school districts, the positive and negative anticipated consequences of such use should be described to policy makers by those test professionals who are closest to the policy before the policy is implemented. *(Secondary)*

Comment:
For example, a common allocation formula involves awarding funds to schools or districts whose mean achievement scores fall below a certain cut score. The use of tests in this way may discourage efforts directed toward higher achievement, since low achievement is being financially rewarded. |

Part III

Standards for Particular Applications

---

13. Testing Linguistic Minorities

Background

For a non-native English speaker and for a speaker of some dialects of English, every test given in English becomes, in part, a language or literacy test. Therefore, testing individuals who have not had substantial exposure to English as it is used in tests presents special challenges. Test results may not reflect accurately the abilities and competencies being measured if test performance depends on these test takers' knowledge of English. Thus special attention may be needed in many aspects of test development, administration, interpretation, and decision making. English language proficiency tests, if appropriately designed and used, are an obvious exception to this concern because they are intended to measure familiarity with English as is required in educational settings.

Individuals who are familiar with two or more languages can vary considerably in their ability to speak, write, comprehend aurally, and read in each language. These abilities are affected by the social or functional situations of communication. Some people may develop socially and culturally acceptable ways of speaking that intermix two or even three languages simultaneously. Some individuals familiar with two languages may perform more slowly, less efficiently, and at times, less accurately, on problem-solving tasks that are administered in the less familiar language. It is important, therefore, to take language background into account in developing, selecting, and administering tests and in interpreting test performance.

In Chapter 1 of the *Standards,* validity is discussed at length. The present chapter extends this discussion, emphasizing the importance of recognizing the limits of interpretations drawn from tests developed without due consideration for the influence of the linguistic characteristics of some test takers.

Tests in Other Languages

Testing in the language of the test takers may sometimes be appropriate. However, there are a number of hazards to be avoided in dual-language tests. One cannot assume that translation produces a version of the test that is equivalent in content, difficulty level, reliability, and validity. Psychometric properties cannot be assumed to be comparable across languages or dialects. Many words have different frequency rates or difficulty levels in different languages or dialects. Therefore, words in two languages that appear to be close in meaning may differ radically in other ways important for the test use intended. Additionally, test content may be inappropriate in a translated version. For example, a test of reading skills in English that is translated to serve as a test of reading skills in Spanish may include content not equally meaningful to Spanish-speaking students.

Language Proficiency Testing

Language tests that can assist in appropriate educational program placement are needed in order to accommodate the large number of people in U.S. schools who have not had sufficient opportunity to learn the English used in schools. The need is particularly pressing in the education of young children but is important also in adult education. In some situations giving tests both in English and in the native language may be necessary to determine the kind of instruction likely to be most beneficial.

Because students are expected to acquire proficiency in English that is appropriate to their ages and educational levels, tests suitable for assessing their progress are needed. Some tests that are prepared for students of English as a foreign language may not be useful if they place insufficient emphasis on the assessment of important listening and speaking skills. Measures of competency in all relevant English language skills (communicative competence, literacy, grammar, pronunciation, and comprehension) are likely to be valuable.

Observing students' speech in naturalistic situations can provide additional information about their proficiency in a language. This may not, however, be sufficient to judge their ability to function in that language in formal situations, such as in the classroom. For example, it is not appropriate to base judgments of a child's ability to benefit from instruction in English solely on language fluency observed in playground speech.

In general, there are special difficulties attendant upon the use of a test with individuals who have not had an adequate opportunity to learn the language of the test. A broader than normal range of tests and observations may be desirable if important decisions are to be based on the test results.

Individual Testing in Schools

Behavior that may appear eccentric or that may be judged negatively in one culture may be appropriate in another. For example, children from some cultures may be reluctant to speak in elaborate language to adults. Children reared in some cultures may be trained to speak to adults only in response to specific questions or with formulaic utterances. Thus, in a testing situation such children may respond to an adult who is probing for elaborate speech with only short phrases or by shrugging their shoulders.

High levels of verbal output is another example of behavior that may have different values across cultures. One group may judge verbosity or rapid speech as rude, whereas another may regard those speech patterns as indications of high mental ability or friendliness. A child from one culture who is evaluated with mores appropriate to another culture may be considered taciturn, withdrawn, or of low mental ability. Resulting interpretations and prescriptions of treatment may be invalid and potentially harmful to the individual being tested.

Standard 13.1

For non-native English speakers or for speakers of some dialects of English, testing should be designed to minimize threats to test reliability and validity that may arise from language differences. *(Primary)*

Comment:
Some tests are inappropriate for use with linguistic minority members whose knowledge of the test language is questionable. Careful professional judgment is required to determine when language differences are relevant. Furthermore, the means by which test users meet this standard will vary with different testing situations. Test users can judge what means are most appropriate to their particular use. Some examples of ways in which this standard might be addressed are as follows:

1. In some group testing situations where many test takers typically come from a particular linguistic minority, the test administration might profitably be conducted by personnel specially trained to interact with members of that group.

2. In many individual assessment situations, such as in clinical testing, a specially trained test administrator may be able to use the test taker's native language or bilingual speech to elicit test responses more effectively. Bilingual communication may be particularly appropriate in testing individuals from groups known to be commonly bilingual (e.g., Chamorro-English speakers from Guam).

3. In individual assessments, the test administrator may also need to be able to take into account language behavior that is considered socially appropriate in the culture of the test taker. For example, slowness or rapidity of response is influenced by culturally learned speech patterns that are known to vary across linguistic groups.

Standard 13.2	**Linguistic modifications recommmended by test publishers should be described in detail in the test manual.** *(Primary)*

Standard 13.3	**When a test is recommended for use with linguistically diverse test takers, test developers and publishers should provide the information necessary for appropriate test use and interpretation.** *(Primary)*

Comment:
Test developers should include in test manuals and in instructions for interpretation explicit statements about the applicability of the test with individuals who are not native speakers of English. However, it should be recognized that test developers and publishers will seldom find it feasible to conduct studies specific to the large number of linguistic groups in this country.

Standard 13.4	**When a test is translated from one language or dialect to another, its reliability and validity for the uses intended in the linguistic groups to be tested should be established.** *(Primary)*

Comment:
For example, if a test is translated into Spanish for use with Mexican and Puerto Rican populations, its reliability and validity should be established with members of each of these groups.

Standard 13.5	**In employment, licensing, and certification testing, the English language proficiency level of the test should not exceed that appropriate to the relevant occupation or profession.** *(Primary)*

Standard 13.6	**When it is intended that the two versions of dual-language tests be comparable, evidence of test comparability should be reported.** *(Primary)*

Standard 13.7	**English language proficiency should not be determined solely with tests that demand only a single linguistic skill.** *(Primary)*

Comment:
For example, a multiple-choice, pencil-and-paper test on vocabulary does not indicate how well a person understands the language when spoken nor how well the person speaks the language. However, the test score might be helpful in determining how well a person understands some aspects of the written language. In making placement decisions, for example, a more complete range of language skills needs to be assessed.

14. Testing People Who Have Handicapping Conditions

Tests are administered to people who have handicapping conditions in a variety of settings and for diverse purposes. There are a number of modifications of tests and test administration procedures that make it possible for people with certain handicapping conditions to take tests developed originally for the general population. Some modified tests, with accompanying research, have been made available by the major national testing programs for a number of years. Although the development of tests and testing procedures for such people is encouraged by the *Standards,* it should be noted that all relevant individual standards given elsewhere in this document are fully applicable to the testing applications considered in this chapter.

Some of the modifications in the way a test is administered alter the medium in which the test instructions and questions are presented to the test takers. For visually impaired people a variety of modifications may be needed. The test booklet may be produced in large print, high-quality regular print, or braille, or the test may be tape-recorded or read aloud to the test taker.

Many hearing-impaired individuals, especially the prelingually deaf, have difficulty in understanding written as well as spoken language; therefore, the intelligibility of the instructions for tests, whether written or spoken, should be considered when tests are modified for hearing-impaired test takers. Modifications of test administration for deaf and hearing-impaired people often include having an interpreter who signs or otherwise interprets the test instructions and, occasionally, the test questions.

The method used to record a response may also need to be modified. Test takers who cannot record their answers to test questions are assisted most commonly by a person who writes or marks the answers. Other ways of obtaining a response include having the respondent use a tape recorder, a typewriter, or a braillewriter. A test may have to be modified to allow a test taker to point to the response of his or her choice.

Nearly all national testing programs that provide modified test procedures for handicapped people provide additional time to take the test. Reading braille and using a cassette recorder or a reader take longer than reading regular print. Reading large type may or may not be more time consuming, depending on the layout of the material and on the nature and severity of the impairment.

Although modifications in the time allowed for tests are considered among the appropriate test options, there are few data available to support any conclusions about the effects of modifications in time, number of sittings, or number of recesses on the test results. Furthermore, little is known about how much time people with various handicapping conditions actually need because records of the time actually used are rare, and empirical studies to set time limits are even more rare.

Changes in test content are sometimes required for test takers with visual or hearing impairments. Items may be unnecessarily difficult for visually impaired people if they use visual stimuli to measure knowledge acquired through other senses. This problem can be identified and corrected by simply reviewing the items, spotting the offenders, and substituting nonvisual stimuli. Because the substitutions may alter other characteristics of the items, however, the modified items should be tried out before they are used in operational testing situations. In certain situations the test may also cause problems if it measures knowledge, skills, or concepts learned primarily through vision.

Verbal tests may create more severe problems for test takers who are prelingually deaf than for those with visual impairments. However, finding appropriate nonverbal tests to measure the same abilities or to predict the same behavior may be extremely difficult. Although this is a testing problem, it reflects more fundamental difficulties in understanding the nature of abilities, what abilities are needed in certain situations, and what existing abilities may compensate for impaired abilities in certain circumstances.

Many of the modifications in the ways tests are administered for handicapped people necessitate that the tests be given individually rather than to groups of respondents. The reasons for having an individual administration include the absence of a practical or convenient way to use a group administration, the desire not to interfere with others taking a test in a group, and the desire to reduce the anxiety handicapped people may have about the test. Some additional alterations may be required: for example, changing the location of the standard testing site if it is not accessible to people in wheelchairs; providing tables or chairs that make test takers with certain physical disabilities more comfortable; and altering lighting conditions and associated space needs for people with some visual impairments.

Despite the history of attempts to modify tests for handicapped people, significant problems remain. First, there have been few empirical investigations of the effects of special accommodations on the resulting scores or on their reliability and validity. Strictly speaking, unless it has been demonstrated that the psychometric properties of a test, or type of test, are not altered significantly by some modification, the claims made for the test by its author or publisher cannot be generalized to the modified version. The major reason for the lack of research is the relatively small number of handicapped test takers. For example, there are usually not enough students with handicapping conditions entering one school in any given year to conduct the type of validation study that is usually conducted for college admission tests.

Although modifying tests for individuals with handicapping conditions is generally regarded as desirable, sometimes some very basic, unanswered questions should be confronted. When tests are administered to people with handicapping conditions, particularly those handicaps that affect cognitive functioning, a relevant question is whether the modified test measures the same constructs. Do changes in the medium of expression affect cognitive functioning and the meaning of responses?

Of all the aspects of testing people who have handicapping conditions, reporting test scores has created the most heated debate. Many test developers have argued that reporting scores from nonstandard test administrations without special identification (often called "flagging" of test scores) violates professional principles, misleads test users, and perhaps even harms handicapped test takers whose scores do not accurately reflect their abilities. Handicapped people, on the other hand, have generally said that to identify their scores as resulting from nonstandard administrations and in so doing to identify them as handicapped is to deny them the opportunity to compete on the same grounds as nonhandicapped test takers, that is, to treat them inequitably. Until test scores can be demonstrated to be comparable in some widely accepted sense, there is little hope of happily resolving from all perspectives the issue of reporting scores with or without special identification. Professional and ethical considerations should be weighed to arrive at a solution, either as an interim measure or as continuing policy.

Standard 14.1	People who modify tests for handicapped people should have available to them psychometric expertise for so doing. In addition, they should have available to them knowledge of the effects of various handicapping conditions on test performance, acquired either from their own training or experience or from close consultation with handicapped individuals or those thoroughly familiar with such individuals. *(Primary)*

Standard 14.2	Until tests have been validated for people who have specific handicapping conditions, test publishers should issue cautionary statements in manuals and elsewhere regarding confidence in interpretations based on such test scores. *(Primary)*

Standard 14.3	Forms of tests that are modified for people who have various handicapping conditions should generally be pilot tested on people who are similarly handicapped to check the appropriateness and feasibility of the modifications. *(Conditional)*

Comment:
Although useful guides to modifying tests are available, they do not provide a universal substitute for trying out a modified test or validating the modified version of a test. Even when such tryouts are conducted on samples inadequate to produce norm or validity data, they should be conducted to check the mechanics of the modifications.

Standard 14.4	Interpretive information that accompanies modified tests should include a careful statement of the steps taken to modify tests in order to alert users to changes that are likely to alter the validity of the measure. *(Conditional)*

Comment:
If empirical evidence of the nature and effects of changes resulting from modifying standard tests is lacking, it is impossible to enumerate significant modifications that are to be documented in manuals. Therefore, test developers should take care to document all changes made and be alert to indications of possible effects of those modifications. Documentation of the procedure used to modify tests will not only aid in the administration and interpretation of the given test but will also inform others who are modifying tests for people with specific handicapping conditions.

Standard 14.5	Empirical procedures should be used whenever possible to establish time limits for modified forms of timed tests rather than simply allowing handicapped test takers a multiple of the standard time. Fatigue should be investigated as a potentially important factor when time limits are extended. *(Secondary)*

Standard 14.6   When feasible, the validity and reliability of tests administered to people with various handicapping conditions should be investigated and reported by the agency or publisher that makes the modification. Such investigations should examine the effects of modifications made for people with various handicapping conditions on resulting scores, as well as the effects of administering standard unmodified tests to them. *(Secondary)*

Comment:
In addition to modifying tests and test administration procedures for people who have handicapping conditions, validating these tests is urgently needed. Validation is the only way to amass knowledge about the usefulness of tests for people with handicapping conditions. The costs of validating these tests should be weighed against those of not having usable information regarding the meanings of scores for handicapped people.

Standard 14.7   Those who use tests and those who interact professionally with potential test takers with handicapping conditions (e.g., high school guidance counselors) should (a) possess the information necessary to make an appropriate selection of alternate measures, (b) have current information regarding the availability of modified forms of the test in question, (c) inform individuals with handicapping conditions, when appropriate, about the existence of modified forms, and (d) make these forms available to test takers when appropriate and feasible. *(Primary)*

Standard 14.8   In assessing characteristics of individuals with handicapping conditions, the test user should use either regular or special norms for calculating derived scores, depending on the purpose of the testing. Regular norms for the characteristic in question are appropriate when the purpose involves the test taker's functioning relative to the general population. If available, however, special norms should be selected when the test takers' functioning relative to their handicapped peers is at issue. *(Primary)*

Part IV

Standards for Administrative Procedures

15. Test Administration, Scoring, and Reporting

Background

Interpretations of test results, like those of experimental results, are most reliable when the measurements are obtained under standardized or controlled conditions. Without standardization, the quality of interpretations will be reduced to the extent that differences in procedure influence performance. To be sure, in some circumstances testing conditions may be changed systematically in order to improve the understanding of an individual's performance. Accurate scoring and reporting are essential in all circumstances. Computerized test administration and reporting can introduce some special difficulties.

Standard 15.1

In typical applications, test administrators should follow carefully the standardized procedures for administration and scoring specified by the test publisher. Specifications regarding instructions to test takers, time limits, the form of item presentation or response, and test materials or equipment should be strictly observed. Exceptions should be made only on the basis of carefully considered professional judgment, primarily in clinical applications. *(Primary)*

Standard 15.2

The testing environment should be one of reasonable comfort and with minimal distractions. Testing materials should be readable and understandable. In computerized testing, items displayed on a screen should be legible and free from glare, and the terminal should be properly positioned. *(Primary)*

Comment:
Testing sessions should be monitored where appropriate both to assist the test taker when a need arises and to maintain proper administrative procedures. Noise, disruption in the testing area, extremes of temperature, inadequate work space, illegible materials, and so forth are among the conditions that should be avoided in testing situations. In the context of computer-administered tests, the novelty of the presentation may have an unknown effect on the test administration.

Standard 15.3

Reasonable efforts should be made to assure the validity of test scores by eliminating opportunities for test takers to attain scores by fraudulent means. *(Primary)*

Comment:
In large-scale testing programs where the results may be viewed as having important consequences, these efforts should include, when appropriate and practicable, simultaneous administration to all individuals taking the same form, stipulating requirements for identification, constructing seating charts, assigning test takers to seats, requiring appropriate space between seats, and providing continuous monitoring of the testing process. Test administrators should note and report any significant instances of testing irregularity.

Standard 15.4

In school situations not involving admissions and in clinical and counseling applications, any modification of standard test administration procedures or scoring should be described in the testing reports with appropriate cautions regarding the possible effects of such modifications on validity. *(Primary)*

Standard 15.5	Test scoring services should document the procedures that were followed in order to assure accuracy of scoring. The frequency of error should be monitored and reported on request. *(Conditional)*

Standard 15.6	When the score report may be the basis on which decisions would be made in the near future and a material error is found in test scores or other important information released by a testing organization or other institution, a corrected score report should be distributed as soon as it is practicable. *(Primary)*

Standard 15.7	Test users should protect the security of test materials. *(Primary)*

Comment:
Those who have test materials under their control should take all steps necessary to assure that only individuals with a legitimate need for access to test materials are able to obtain such access.

Standard 15.8	In educational admissions and licensing or certification applications, in which important decisions depend on performance on a given test, a means of checking the accuracy of the scoring should be available to test takers. When the test itself and the scoring key cannot be released, some other means of verification should be provided. *(Conditional)*

Standard 15.9	When test data about a person are retained, both the test protocol and any written report should also be preserved. *(Primary)*

Standard 15.10	Those responsible for testing programs should provide appropriate interpretations when test score information is released to students, parents, legal representatives, teachers, or the media. The interpretations should describe in simple language what the test covers, what scores mean, common misinterpretations of test scores, and how scores will be used. *(Primary)*

Comment:
Test users should consult the interpretive material prepared by the test developer or publisher and should revise or supplement the material as necessary to present the local and individual results accurately and clearly.

Standard 15.11	Organizations that maintain test scores on individuals in data files or in an individual's records should develop a clear set of policy guidelines on the duration of retention in an individual's records, availability, and use over time of such scores. *(Primary)*

Comment:
In some instances test scores become obsolete over time and should not be used or be available. In other cases test scores obtained in past years can be extremely useful, for example, in longitudinal assessment. The key issue is the valid use of the information.

16. Protecting the Rights of Test Takers

Background

Certain broad principles regarding access to test scores are now widely accepted. Some technical requirements necessary to satisfy these principles are stated as specific standards in this chapter. The issues of test security and the cancellation of test takers' scores because of testing irregularities are also addressed.

Standard 16.1

Informed consent should be obtained from test takers or their legal representatives before testing is done except (a) when testing without consent is mandated by law or governmental regulation (e.g., statewide testing programs); (b) when testing is conducted as a regular part of school activities (e.g., schoolwide testing programs and participation by schools in norming and research studies); or (c) when consent is clearly implied (e.g., application for employment or educational admissions). When consent is not required, test takers should be informed concerning the testing process. *(Primary)*

Comment:
Informed consent implies that the test takers or representatives are made aware, in language that they can understand, of the reasons for testing, the type of tests to be used, the intended use and the range of material consequences of the intended use, and what testing information will be released and to whom. When law mandates testing but does not require informed consent, test users should exercise discretion in obtaining informed consent, but test takers should always be given relevant information about a test when it is in their interest to be informed.

Young test takers should receive an explanation of the reasons for testing. Even a child as young as two or three and many mentally retarded test takers can understand a simple explanation as to why they are being tested. For example, an explanation such as "I'm going to ask you to try to do some things so that I can see what you know how to do and what things you could use some more help with" would be understandable to such test takers.

Standard 16.2

In school, clinical, and counseling applications, test users should provide test takers or their legal representative with an appropriate explanation of test results and recommendations made on the basis of test results in a form that they can understand. *(Primary)*

Comment:
This standard requires both the use of the appropriate language with non-English speaking test takers and the use of conceptually understandable explanations with all types of test takers. Even children and many mentally retarded test takers can understand a simple explanation of test results.

Standard 16.3

Test results identified by the names of individual test takers should not be released to any person or institution without the informed consent of the test taker or an authorized representative unless otherwise required by law. Scores of individuals identified by name should be made

available only to those with a legitimate, professional interest in particular cases. *(Primary)*

Comment:
Information may be provided to researchers if a test taker's anonymity is maintained and the intended use is not inconsistent with the conditions of the test taker's informed consent.

Standard 16.4	In educational, clinical, and counseling applications, when test scores are used to make decisions about individuals, the affected person or legal representative should be able to obtain transmittal of this test score and its interpretation for any appropriate use. *(Secondary)*

Standard 16.5	Test data maintained in data files should be adequately protected from improper disclosure. Use of time-sharing networks, data banks, and other electronic data processing systems should be restricted to situations in which confidentiality can be reasonably assured. *(Primary)*

Standard 16.6	When score reporting includes assigning individuals to categories, the categories chosen should be based on carefully selected criteria. The least stigmatizing labels, consistent with accurate reporting, should always be assigned. *(Primary)*

Standard 16.7	Under certain conditions it may be desirable to cancel a test taker's score or to withhold it because of possible testing irregularities, including suspected misconduct. The type of evidence and procedures to be used to determine that a score should be canceled or withheld should be explained fully to all test takers whose scores are being withheld or canceled. *(Primary)*

Standard 16.8	In educational admissions and licensing and certification applications, when a score report will be delayed beyond a brief investigative period because of possible irregularities such as suspected misconduct, the test taker should be notified, the reason given, and reasonable efforts made to expedite review and to protect the interests of the test taker. *(Primary)*

Standard 16.9	In educational admissions and licensing and certification applications, before a score is canceled or its report is withheld beyond a brief investigative period, test takers should be given advance warning and an opportunity to provide evidence that the score should not be canceled or withheld. All evidence considered in deciding upon the intended action, including evidence that might lead to a contrary decision, should be made available to the test taker on request. *(Primary)*

Comment:
Some testing organizations offer the option of a prompt and free retest or arbitration of disputes.

Standard 16.10   **In educational admissions and licensing and certification applications, when testing irregularities are suspected, all available data judged to be relevant should be considered.** *(Primary)*

Comment:
Allegations of testing irregularity that involve copying are sometimes based on a comparison of the distractors chosen by two test takers on items answered incorrectly by both. This method should not be used as the sole basis for decisions since it ignores other evidence that might indicate that copying did not take place. Reasonable efforts should be made to obtain contrary, as well as supporting, evidence to settle the matter of irregularity as well as the validity of the questioned score.

Glossary

For many of the terms defined in this glossary, multiple definitions can be found in the literature. The following definitions indicate how each term is used in this text.

ability test A test that measures the current performance or estimates future performance of a person in some defined domain of cognitive, psychomotor, or physical functioning. See also *aptitude test* and *achievement test.*

achievement test A test that measures the extent to which a person commands a certain body of information or possesses a certain skill, usually in a field where training or instruction has been received. See also *ability test* and *aptitude test.*

adaptive testing A sequential form of testing in which successive items in the test are chosen based on the responses to previous items.

alternate forms Two or more forms that are similar in nature and intended for the same purpose. There are three categories of alternate forms. Comparable forms are similar in nature but have not been demonstrated to have similar statistical characteristics. For forms to be called parallel, the means, standard deviations, and correlations with other measures should be considered approximately equal. For forms to be called equivalent, they should be the same in all characteristics that matter.

anchor test A common set of items administered with each of two or more different forms of a test for the purpose of equating the scores of these forms.

aptitude test A test that estimates future performance on other tasks not necessarily having evident similarity to the test tasks. Aptitude tests are often aimed at indicating an individual's readiness to learn or to develop proficiency in some particular area if education or training is provided. Aptitude tests sometimes do not differ in form or substance from achievement tests, but may differ in use and interpretation. See also *ability test* and *achievement test.*

assessment procedure Any method used to measure characteristics of people, programs, or objects.

attenuation The reduction of a correlation or regression coefficient from its theoretical true value due to the imperfect reliability of one or both measures entering into the relationship.

battery A set of tests standardized on the same population, so that norm-referenced scores on the several tests can be compared or used in combination for decision making.

classification The act of determining which of several possible assignments or treatments a person is to receive or is advised to choose.

coaching Planned short-term instructional activities in which prospective test takers participate prior to the test administration for the primary purpose of increasing their test scores. Coaching typically includes simple practice, instruction on test-taking strategies, and so forth. Activities that approximate the instruction provided by regular school curricula or training programs are not typically referred to as coaching.

comparable scores Scores on different tests expressed on the same scale and having the same relative meaning within some common reference group.

competency test An achievement test that measures the level of skill or knowledge possessed by test takers in relation to some defined domain of skills or knowledge.

composite score A score that combines several scores by a specified formula.

computer-based interpretation A method of providing test score interpretations that rely on computer algorithms and computer-printed score reports, with narrative statements.

concurrent criterion-related evidence of validity Evidence of criterion-related validity in which predictor and criterion information are obtained at approximately the same time.

conditional standards Standards that are considered primary for some situations and secondary for others. In deciding whether to take an individual conditional standard as primary or secondary, one should consider carefully the feasibility of meeting that standard in relation to the potential consequences to all parties involved in the testing process. It may be infeasible technically or financially for some testing programs to observe some conditional standards, particularly those programs that conduct low-volume tests. However, if the use of the test is likely to have serious consequences for test takers, especially if a large number of people may be affected, the conditional standard assumes increased importance.

confidence interval The points on a score scale that define, with specified probability, an interval that includes the parameter of interest. The term is also used in these standards to designate Bayesian credibility intervals that define the probability that the unknown parameter falls in the specified interval.

configural scoring rule A rule used for assigning weights to paired variables so that the interpretation of one predictor score depends upon the level of the second predictor score.

construct A psychological characteristic (e.g., numerical ability, spatial ability, introversion, anxiety) considered to vary or differ across individuals. A construct (sometimes called a latent variable) is not directly observable; rather it is a theoretical concept derived from research and other experience that has been constructed to explain observable behavior patterns. When test scores are interpreted by using a construct, the scores are placed in a conceptual framework.

construct-related evidence of validity Evidence that supports a proposed construct interpretation of scores on a test based on theoretical implications associated with the construct label.

content domain A body of knowledge, skills, and abilities defined so that items of knowledge or particular tasks can be clearly identified as included or excluded from the domain.

content-related evidence of validity Evidence that shows the extent to which the content domain of a test is appropriate relative to its intended purpose. Such evidence is used to establish that the test includes a representative or critical sample of the relevant content domain and that it excludes content outside that domain. In employment selection testing, the content domain consists of tasks, knowledge, skills, and abilities associated with a job. In educational achievement testing, the content domain refers to the content of the curriculum, the actual instruction, or the objectives of the instruction.

criterion An indicator of the accepted value of outcome performance, such as grade-point average, productivity rate, accident rate, performance rate, absenteeism rate, reject rate, and so forth. It is usually a standard against which a predictive measure is evaluated.

criterion-referenced test A test that allows its users to make score interpretations in relation to a functional performance level, as distinguished from those interpretations that are made in relation to the performance of others. See also *domain-referenced test*.

criterion-related evidence of validity Evidence that shows the extent to which scores on a test are related to a criterion measure.

critical score level A pivotal point on a test score scale above and below which decisions and evaluations differ. See also *cut score*.

cross-validation Applying an empirically derived scoring system or set of weights from one sample to a second sample in order to investigate the stability of prediction of the scoring system or weights.

cut score A specified point on a score scale at or above which candidates pass or are accepted and below which candidates fail or are rejected. (The decision to accept or reject may be subject to revision in light of further information.) See also *critical score level*.

decision consistency The percentage of times that the same decision is made when a specified decision rule is used across alternate testings, assuming no changes have occurred in the true abilities of the test takers.

decision rule A rule for choosing a course of action on the basis of evidence. For example, a rule by which teachers pass or fail students in a course based on students' test scores and other performance in a course; a rule by which a government agency ranks project proposals for funding based on the contents of the proposals and the ratings assigned to them by judges; or a rule by which an evaluator decides that the difference among the test scores of students who are exposed to different programs has practical significance.

derived score A score to which raw scores are converted by numerical transformation (e.g., percentile ranks or standard scores).

differential prediction The degree to which a test that is used to predict people's relative attainments yields different predictions for the same criteria among groups with different demographic characteristics, prior experience, or treatment.

discrimination The ability of a test or a test item to differentiate among individuals by measuring the extent to which the individuals display the attribute that is being measured by that test or item.

documentation The body of literature (e.g., test manuals, manual supplements, research reports, publications, etc.) made available to support test use.

domain-referenced test A test that allows users to estimate the amount of a specified content domain that an individual has learned. Domains may be based on sets of instructional objectives, for example. See also *criterion-referenced tests* and *content-related evidence of validity*.

domain sampling The process of selecting test items to represent the specific universe of performance in which a test developer is interested.

equated forms Two or more test forms that yield equivalent or parallel scores for specified groups of test takers.

equating method A process used to convert the score scale of one form of test to the score scale of another form so that the scores are equivalent or parallel.

equipercentile equating An equating method that defines equivalent scores as scores having the same percentile rank in each distribution.

equivalent forms See *alternate forms*.

error of measurement The difference between an observed score and the corresponding true score. See also *standard error of measurement* and *true score*.

expectancy table A table of discrete values used for making predictions of levels of criterion performance for specified values or in specified intervals of predictor scores.

expected growth The average amount of change in test scores that occurs over a specified time interval for individuals with certain individual characteristics such as age or grade level.

factor In measurement theory, a derived, hypothetical dimension that accounts for part of the intercorrelations among tests. Strictly, the term refers to a mathematical dimension constructed by a factor analysis, but it is also commonly used to denote the psychological construct associated with the dimension, for example, an attribute such as verbal ability (verbal factor) or numerical ability (numerical factor).

factor analysis Any of several methods of analyzing the intercorrelations or covariances among variables by constructing hypothetical factors, which are fewer in number than the original variables. It indicates how much of the variation in each original measure can be accounted for by each of the hypothetical factors.

false negative In selection, an error in which a person is predicted to fail, but would have succeeded if selected. Alternatively, classifying someone incorrectly as being in a lower group.

false positive In selection, an error in which a person is predicted to succeed, but would have failed if selected. Alternatively, classifying someone incorrectly as being in a higher group.

feasible Capable of being done successfully given practical constraints.

free response A response to a test item that the test taker must supply, as opposed to a response that the test taker must select from a list of alternatives.

gain scores The difference between the score on a test and the score on an earlier administration of the same test or an equivalent one.

generalizability theory An extension of classical reliability theory and methodology in which analysis of variance is used to estimate variance components and hence to describe the magnitude of errors from specified sources. The analysis is used to evaluate the generalizability of scores beyond the specific sample of items, persons, and observational conditions that were studied.

grade equivalent score The grade level for which a given score is the real or estimated median or mean.

informed consent The granting of consent by the test taker to be tested on the basis of full information concerning the purpose of the testing, the persons who may receive the test scores, the use to which the test score may be put, and such other information as may be material to the consent process.

internal analysis (of reliability) A class of methods for estimating reliability based on the administration of a single test form. Members of the class include coefficient alpha, Kuder-Richardson formulas, and methods involving internal splits of the test.

inter-rater reliability Consistency of judgments made about people or objects among raters or sets of raters.

interest inventory A set of questions or statements that is used to infer the interests, preferences, likes, and dislikes of a respondent.

interpretive report A summary of test scores and associated information that provides meaningful interpretation of the scores.

inventory A questionnaire or checklist, usually in the form of a self-report, that elicits information about an individual. Inventories are not tests in the strict sense; they are most often concerned with personality characteristics, interests, attitudes, preferences, personal problems, motivation, and so forth.

item analysis The process of assessing certain characteristics of test items, usually the difficulty value, the discriminating power, and sometimes, the correlation with an external criterion.

item bias An item is considered positively or negatively biased for a group within a population if (a) the average expected item score for that group is substantially higher or lower than that for the overall population and (b) if this disparity stems from factors that the item is not intended to measure rather than from factors it is intended to measure.

item difficulty index An index that indicates the percentage of people in some specified group, such as students of a given age, grade, or ability level, that answers a test item correctly.

item discrimination index A measure of the extent to which test takers who are judged to be high in terms of some criterion exhibit higher performance on an item than do those who are judged to be low on the same criterion.

item response curve A function relating the probability of success on an item to the level of the attribute measured by the item (also called item characteristic curve).

job analysis Any of several methods of identifying the tasks performed on a job or the knowledge, skills, and abilities required to perform that job.

longitudinal study Research that involves the measurement of a single sample at several different points in time.

low-volume test In these standards, a test for which the number of test takers is too small to permit undertaking those data analyses specified in conditional standards. For standards applying to subgroup analyses, this definition will apply to each subgroup sample. Determining whether a test is high or low volume involves careful professional judgment; for purposes of individual conditional standards, this judgment may vary.

normative Pertaining to norms or norm groups.

norms Statistics or tabular data that summarize the test performance of specified groups, such as test takers of various ages or grades. Norms are often assumed to represent some larger population, such as test takers throughout the country.

norm-referenced test An instrument for which interpretation is based on the comparison of a test taker's performance to the performance of other people in a specified group.

objectives-referenced test See *domain-referenced test*.

out-of-level testing Administering a test that is designed primarily for people of an age or grade level above or below that of the test taker.

parallel forms See *alternate forms*.

percentile The score on a test below which a given percentage of scores fall.

percentile rank The percentage of scores in a specified distribution that fall at or below the point at which a given score lies.

personality inventory An inventory that measures one or more characteristics that are regarded generally as psychological attributes or interpersonal skills.

predictive bias The systematic under- or over-prediction of criterion performance for people belonging to groups differentiated by characteristics not relevant to criterion performance.

predictive criterion-related evidence of validity Evidence of criterion-related validity in which criterion scores are observed at a later date, for example, for job or school performance.

predictor A measurable characteristic that predicts criterion performance such as scores on a test, evidence of previous performance, and judgments of interviewers, panels, or raters.

primary standards Standards that should be met by all tests before their operational use and in all test uses, unless a sound professional reason is available to show why it is not necessary, or technically feasible, to do so in a particular case. Test developers and users and, where appropriate, sponsors, are expected to be able to explain why any primary standards have not been met.

prior information Any pertinent information that is available before observations are collected for a study.

profile A graphic representation of an individual's scores (or their relative magnitudes) on several tests that employ a single standard scale. See also *battery*.

projective technique A method of personality assessment in which the test taker provides free responses to a series of stimuli such as inkblots, pictures, or incomplete sentences. The term reflects the assumption that people project into their responses their perceptions, feelings, and styles. Also called projective method.

psychometric Pertaining to the measurement of psychological characteristics such as abilities, aptitudes, achievement, personality traits, skill, and knowledge.

raw score The unadjusted score on a test, usually determined by counting the number of correct answers, but sometimes determined by subtracting a fraction of the wrong answers from the number of correct answers. See also *scoring formula*.

reliability The degree to which test scores are consistent, dependable, or repeatable, that is, the degree to which they are free of errors of measurement.

reliability coefficient A coefficient of correlation between two administrations of a test. The conditions of administration may involve variation in test forms, raters or scorers, or passage of time. These and other changes in conditions give rise to qualifying adjectives being used to describe the particular coefficient, e.g. parallel form reliability, rater reliability, test retest reliability, etc.

replication Repeating an observation or study under the same conditions in order to investigate the stability of the results.

residual score The difference between the observed and the true or predicted score.

restriction of range A situation in which, because of sampling restrictions, the variability of data in the sample is less than the variability in the population of interest.

scaled score See *derived score*.

score Any specific number resulting from the assessment of an individual; a generic term applied for convenience to such diverse measures as test scores, estimates of latent variables, production counts, absence records, course grades, ratings, and so forth.

scoring formula The formula by which the raw score on a test is obtained. The simplest scoring formula is "raw score equals number correct." Other formulas weight different item responses differently, sometimes in an attempt to correct for guessing or nonresponse, by assigning zero weights to nonresponses and negative weights to incorrect responses.

screening test A test that is used to make broad categorizations as a first step in selection decisions or diagnostic processes.

secondary standards Standards that are desirable as goals but are likely to be beyond reasonable expectation in many situations. Although careful consideration of these standards will often help in evaluating tests and programs and in comparing the usefulness of competing instruments, limitations on resources may make adherence to them infeasible in many situations. Some secondary standards describe procedures that are beneficial but not often used. Test developers and users are not expected to be able to explain why secondary standards have not been met.

selection decision A two-alternative classification decision in which rejection is one possible assignment or treatment.

selection bias See *predictive bias*.

simultaneous estimation A procedure (classical, Bayesian, or empirical Bayesian) for estimating two or more values simultaneously. The objective is to improve the estimation of each parameter by using information jointly gathered for the entire class of values.

speed test A test in which performance is measured by the number of tasks performed in a given time. Examples are tests of typing speed and reading speed. Also, a test scored for accuracy where the test taker works under time pressure.

speededness The extent to which a test taker's score on a test depends on the rate at which work is performed rather than on the correctness of the response. One index of speededness is the percentage of test takers who do not complete the test.

split-half reliability coefficient An internal analysis coefficient obtained by using half the items on the test to yield one score and the other half of the items to yield a second, independent score. The correlation between the scores on these two half-tests, stepped up via the Spearman-Brown Formula, provides an estimate of the alternate-form reliability of the total test.

standard error of estimate A summary statistic that conveys the average of the magnitude of errors of prediction that is associated with using a regression equation to predict Y, given X.

standard error of measurement The standard deviation of errors of measurement that is associated with the test scores for a specified group of test takers.

standard score A score that describes the location of a person's score within a set of scores in terms of its distance from the mean in standard deviation units.

technical manuals Booklets prepared by test publishers to provide technical information on a test.

test manuals Booklets prepared by test publishers and others to provide information on test administration, scoring, and interpretation and to provide technical data on test characteristics and procedures that are used in test development, and in reliability and validity studies.

test-retest coefficient A reliability coefficient obtained by administering the same test a second time to the same group after a time interval and correlating the two sets of scores.

T-score A derived score on a scale having a mean score of 50 units and a standard deviation of 10 units.

test specifications A content outline that specifies what proportion of the items shall deal with each content area and with each type of ability. The outline may also include specifications such as the number of items in the test, the time to be allowed for its administration, the typical format of items, and statistical specifications such as distributions of item difficulty and discrimination indices.

true score In classical test theory, the average of the scores earned by an individual on an unlimited number of perfectly parallel forms of the same test.

unidimensionality A characteristic of a test that measures only one latent variable.

user's guide A statement of the purpose of a test, its content, and appropriate uses, together with information on test administration, scoring, normative data, and interpretation of results. Often this is a subset of the material in the test manual.

utility The relative value of an outcome with respect to a set of other possible outcomes.

validation The process of investigation by which the degree of validity of a proposed test interpretation can be evaluated.

validity The degree to which a certain inference from a test is appropriate or meaningful.

validity coefficient A coefficient of correlation that shows the strength of the relation between predictor and criterion.

validity generalization Applying validity evidence obtained in one or more situations to other similar situations on the basis of simultaneous estimation, meta-analysis, or synthetic validation arguments.

variable   A quantity that may take on any one of a specified set of values.

variance   A measure of variability; the average squared deviation from the mean; the square of the standard deviation.

variance components   Variances of the separate constituent parts that are assumed to be combined in the observed score. Such variances, estimated by methods of the analysis of variance, often reflect situation, location, time, form, rater, and related effects.

weighted scoring   Scoring in which the number of points awarded for a correct (or diagnostically relevant) response is not the same for all items in the test. In some cases, the scoring formula awards more points for one response to an item than for another.

Z-score   A type of standard score scale in which the mean equals zero and the standard deviation equals one unit for the group used in defining the scale.

Bibliography

American Association of Collegiate Registrars and Admissions Officers & American Council on Education. (1978, April). Admissions tests. In *Recruitment admissions and handicapped students. A guide for compliance with Section 504 of the Rehabilitation Act of 1973*. Washington, DC: Author.

American Personnel and Guidance Association. (1980). *Responsibilities of users of standardized tests*. Falls Church, VA: Author.

American Psychological Association. (1954). *Technical recommendations for psychological tests and diagnostic techniques*. Washington, DC: Author.

American Psychological Association. (1966a). Automated test scoring and interpretation practices. In Proceedings of the American Psychological Association. *American Psychologist, 21*(12), 1141.

American Psychological Association. (1966b). *Standards for educational and psychological tests and manuals*. Washington, DC: Author.

American Psychological Association. (1974). *Standards for educational and psychological tests*. Washington, DC: Author.

American Psychological Association. (1977). Guidelines for nonsexist language in APA journals. American Psychologist, *32*(6), 487-494.

American Psychological Association. (1977). Standards for providers of psychological services. *American Psychologist, 32*(6), 495-505.

American Psychological Association. (1981). Ethical principles of psychologists. *American Psychologist, 36*(6), 633-638.

American Psychological Association. (in press). *Ethical principles in the conduct of research with human participants*. Washington, DC: Author.

Association for Measurement and Evaluation in Guidance. (1980, October). *Statement on legislation affecting testing for selection in educational and occupational programs*.

College Entrance Examination Board. (1981). *Guidelines on the uses of College Board test scores and related data*. New York: Author.

Colorado Psychological Association. (1982, January). *Guidelines for use of computerized testing services*.

Department of Health, Education, and Welfare. (1977). Nondiscrimination on basis of handicap in programs and activities receiving or benefiting from federal financial assistance. *Federal Register, 42,*(86), 22676-22702.

Division of Industrial and Organizational Psychology. (1980). *Principles for the validation and use of personnel selection procedures* (2nd ed.). Berkeley, CA: American Psychological Association.

Education for All Handicapped Children Act of 1975, 20 U.S.C. s 1401-1461 (1976).

Educational Testing Service. (1983). *Standards for quality and fairness*. Princeton, NJ: Author.

Equal Employment Opportunity Commission, Civil Service Commission, Department of Labor, & Department of Justice. (1978). Adoption by four agencies of uniform guidelines on employee selection procedures. *Federal Register, 43*(166), 38290-38315.

Equal Employment Opportunity Commission, Office of Personnel Management, Department of Justice, Department of Labor, & Department of the Treasury. (1979). Adoption of questions and answers to clarify and provide a common interpretation of the uniform guidelines on employee selection procedures. *Federal Register, 44*(43), 11996-12009.

Equal Employment Opportunity Commission, Office of Personnel Management, Department of Justice, Department of the Treasury, & Department of Labor Office of Federal Contract Compliance Programs. (1980). Adoption of additional questions and answers to clarify and provide a common interpretation of the uniform guidelines on employee selection procedures. *Federal Register, 45*(87), 29530-29531.

Evaluation Research Society, Inc. (1982). Standards for program evaluation. In P. H. Rossi (Ed.), *New directions for program evaluation* (pp. 37-48). San Francisco: Jossey-Bass.

Heller, K., Holtzman, W., & Messick, S. (1982). *Placing children in special education: A strategy for equity*. Washington, DC: National Academy Press.

Joint AERA, APA, NCME Committee for Review of the Standards for Educational and Psychological Tests. (1979). *Report of the joint AERA, APA, NCME committee for review of the standards for educational and psychological tests*. Washington, DC: Author.

Joint Committee on Standards for Educational Evaluation. (1981). *Standards for evaluations of educational programs, projects, and materials*. New York: McGraw-Hill.

National Council on Measurement in Education Board of Directors. (1980, April). *NCME statement on educational admissions testing*. Washington, DC: Author.

National Education Association. (1955). *Technical recommendations for achievement tests.* Washington, DC: Author.

National Education Association. (1981). Resolutions of the National Education Association. In *Handbook of the National Education Association 1981-1982.* Washington, DC: Author.

National Institute of Education. (1974, July). *Guidelines for assessment of sex bias and sex fairness in career interest inventories.* Washington, DC: Department of Health, Education, and Welfare.

Sherman, S. W., & Robinson, N. M. (Eds.). (1982). *Ability testing of handicapped people: Dilemma for government, science, and the public,* Washington, DC: National Academy Press.

Wigdor, A. K., & Garner, W. R. (Eds.). (1982). *Ability testing: Uses, consequences, and controversies* (Vols 1 & 2). Washington, DC: National Academy Press.

Index

The numbers refer to standards. The digits to the left of the decimal are the chapter numbers. The digits following the decimal are the standard numbers.